THE BANGKOK WORLD

Bluefoot Books

Copyright 2013 Denis E. Horgan
ISBN 978-1-62620-176-7
Photography copyright 2013 William A. Harting
Printed in the United States of America. 2013. Bluefoot Books is an entity of
Bluefoot Entertainment, Inc. West Hartford CT 06107
Bluefoot Books, 977 Farmington Ave., West Hartford, CT 06107
Library of Congress Cataloguing-in-Publication Data
Horgan, Denis Edward
The Bangkok World
First edition
p.cm
ISBN 978-1-62620-176-7
Horgan, Denis Edward, Authors, American -- 21st Century --
Non-Fiction. I. Title.
CIP pending

ใครใคร่ค้าม

ใครใคร่ค้าช

ในนามงปลา

ค้า

ค้า

ในนามขาว

THE BANGKOK WORLD

Denis Horgan

Photography by
William Harting

THE BANGKOK WORLD

Photography by William Harting

OUTSIDE THE PLANE WINDOW the sunrise began to illuminate Asia, miles below us, to the color of a dusty grapeleaf. Shortly, it seemed, we descended over Thailand and found ourselves stepping from the Boeing 707 onto a rolling staircase and into the soup of heat and smells of Bangkok's little Don Muang Airport. It was March of 1969 and the five of us, me, wife Diane and three little daughters, had sold most of our goods and moved – forever, as far as we knew – from Boston into the world.

Of course the three girls, aged nine months, twenty-three months and four years, had little part in the decision-making. They trusted us. After twenty-four hours in the air, we landed a day ahead of the time in Boston, would we ever catch up?

We were assaulted immediately by the heat – it felt like a blast from the wrong side of an air conditioner – and the smells, the perfume of flowers, of water, of decay, of spices, all part of the strange new world we were to inhabit.

It was with my background as a production editor and erstwhile reporter that I entered this new world, where new experiences seared me like the hot peppers that are such a part of the food we would embrace here. This new world, as it turned out, was quite an old new world. Yes, there was electricity, and, thankfully, air conditioning, but the plant where I found myself a day or two later as managing editor of The Bangkok World was antiquated beyond anything I'd experienced. On the other hand, I understood and was absorbed by it immediately.

Though we moved on after what now seems a short while, we really never left.

Wharton

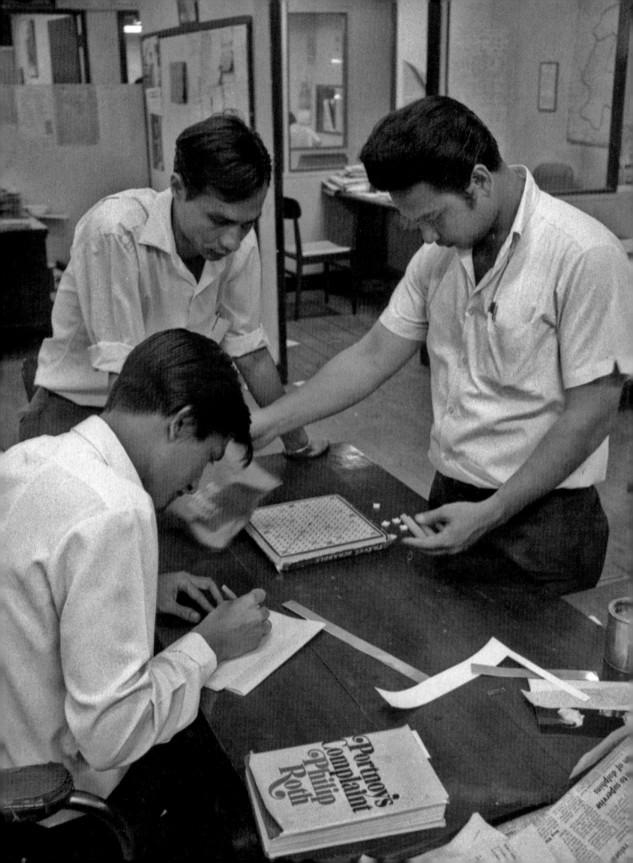

THE BANGKOK WORLD

by Denis Horgan

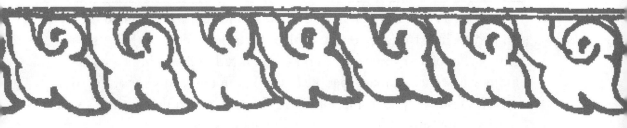

Footnotes & Footprints

NOT SO LONG AGO, sitting at a wobbly streetside table outside a little Bangkok soda shop, I looked across the busy street, wavering as it was in the dragon-breath mirage blur of the unending season's great, embracing, welcoming, under-your-shirt heat, the dazzling sunshine bursting back from scores of gold-tipped stupa spires and soundlessly hissing mosaic nagas, twinkly greens and scratchy reds spiking up over a whitewashed wall crenellated by hundreds of pure white aces of spades, encompassing the very Grand indeed Palace and the incomparable Wat Phra Kaew where garudas play ring-around-the-rosie and gigantic, fierce and Chinese-looking stone warriors, oddly in Fred Astaire top hats, loom to guard the sea of treasures of ancient Thai royalty, of even more ancient Buddhist faith and reverence. Down the little avenue outside, in front of me, small open-air taxis, samlors, or *tuk-tuks*, coughed past in their own blues and reds and rust-browns and dented chrome-silvers stewing the air with an exhausting fog which surely must be bad for us but which is irreplaceably, as much as is all that gilding, a rich part of the amazing exoticism of this majestic place, Krung Thep Mahanakhon Amon Rattanakosin Mahinthara Ayuthaya Mahadilok Phop Noppharat Ratchathani Burirom Udomratchaniwet Mahasathan Amon Piman Awatan Sathit Sakkathattiya Witsanukam Prasit. Krung Thep. Bangkok.

There, as flocks of young Thai school children in cloud-white shirts and coal-black trousers or loose blue skirts giggled by in their astonishing chocolate-eyed beauty, and as great red or green buses burped along with twice as many people aboard than made any sense for comfort in these octopus tropics, and as a fruit vendor called out the sweet merits of the small triangles of pineapple on twigs from his little stand, and as a pedal cart exploding rush brooms and feathery brushes slid by, there I watched with such pride and soft happiness as my young son, Daniel, happened to walk along on the other side of the street, taller than those around him, blonder and more pastel by far, sky-blue-eyed. Away from the rest of us for a moment, he was wanderingly exploring in his way and I smiled at how his mother's beauty so salvaged the mix and how fair he was, and how slim, as if constructed out of Q-tips and pipe cleaners. A young man then only in his early twenties, thin and innocently out of his place, he strolled along in his comfortable confidence, a giraffe to the flow of the smaller Thais around him. I smiled again. Look at him. A kid. A youth. Just a boy. Squeezed, like a bar of soap in the shower, he had landed from his New England haunts in this wondrous place, likely just as alien as those puttin' on the Ritz stone warriors within, but so, so much younger and fresher as well.

Shaking my head, I thought, too, "Was that me? He looks like I must have looked."

Truly a generation earlier than this family visit, hadn't I travelled those very same toasty sidewalks exactly like that? In my early twenties. Slim, as I recall distantly being. Pink and blond where so very few others around me were. A kid. A youth. Just a boy.

Except it was such a far different time. A great war scalded the fantastically lovely region just beyond Thailand's elephant-head margins, and occasionally within, as well. Vast drama played out across

the cultures; diplomacies writhed to no end knowable to anyone not
an insider playing that particularly winless sport; economies soared
and flattened on international developments, worldwide conflicts, on
seeming whimsy; peoples' existences ended violently and no one could
convincingly explain quite why; ancient ways of life collided with
new ones like carnival cars, except with so much more consequence;
opportunity such as can never quite exist again in that special way
opened up, winked shut: opportunities for adventure, for involvement, for escape, for joy, fascination, mayhem and anxiety all together.
Great grown-up games were being played – and somehow, amazingly,
I was part of them.

At Daniel's same easy age of that later visit I was back then a minor
Army officer in a great conflict where people were upended by the
tens of millions, some, inescapably, as a result of my own obscure
accomplishments in uniform. People saluted me, ultimately a young
captain, when no one saluted me before or has since – or has seen any
particular reason to do so. People somehow even younger than I was
and even many quite older, wiser and more knowledgeable by far, did
what I told them to do, for no other reason than because of tiny bits of
metal stuck to my shirt.

A few years later – but still younger than were Daniel's older brothers when they also joined us for them to see Bangkok, for them to first
sample this great, chaotic, amazing, woozying, beguiling, baffling
city's fascinations – I was barely believably the lofty editor and even
more incomprehensibly the publisher of an English-language newspaper in Bangkok, Thailand, a newspaper to which people actually
turned each day for important information and advice and diversion.
In my mid-twenties, it was my job to guide a newspaper staff made up
of all manner of rascals and geniuses, daffy people and hard-working
souls, harder-drinking wizards and crooks, poets, adventurers, exiles,

wanderers. Only rarely had many of them been journalists before becoming part of the Bangkok World, but "journalist" was a title I could bestow somehow with all the breezy authority of a knighting, sword-tapping monarch assigning some mindless suit of armor a duchy or lordship. If we said they were newspaper people, they were newspaper people. The role put me in the elbow-rubbing company of emissaries of distant communities which I could barely find on a map; beribboned government officials with so many medals and distinctions upon them that they rattled when they walked grimly took me into account; I was part of important decisions where grand commercial and cultural details minnow-skittered about, nearly as lost to me as if they were all in Mandarin or Tagalog, or in Thai, a symphony of a language which I never was able to master; because of the seat I sat on I was a lion cub in a social expatriate menagerie that had mounted few wise rules to restrict such as me from mysteriously being there. I was doing work for which I had truly never been trained but which I carried off with vast flair and faux authority, a style of rich self-assurance, a card-sharp's nimbleness as a dodge to ever having to concede aloud that I had so little genuine idea at all of what mischief I was up to – or into.

How could that have ever happened?

Well, like most things, it happened of course by mad accident and gnarled coincidences and happy luck. At twenty-four, actually old by the carnivorous standard of the uniform, the military had sent me to Southeast Asia to help lose the great Indochina war it was so bloodily muddling along in there. I did my best, which is maybe more than can be claimed by some in the Army's stellar heights or around the nation's cold-blooded leadership tables who created the carnage out of thin air. They even gave me medals to show for it as souvenirs. At twenty-six, I re-donned the mufti and became a newspaper bigwig. In Bangkok, Thailand. This may seem far and away from the more traditional realms of bigwiggery, but undoubtedly few publishing moguls elsewhere can make claim to such experiences and memories as were inspired wringing an English-language newspaper out of the merrily unruly Land of Smiles. It was a newsroom of pirates and passing-through adventurers, runaways and rock-solid locals, drifters and professionals alike, and others, too, mostly quietly reflecting sixteen different nations which so often otherwise had little time for another; but worldwide differences in skills and backgrounds meshed and, with that, we did such a very good job. And I was the boss.

Imagine that.

If I had ever set out to chart a route that would take me from the triple-decker Dorchester tenements in one of Boston's several vibrant, Only Irish Need Apply neighborhoods, even my remarkably fevered imagination wouldn't have come up with such a back-moonside desti-nation as the lovely Phrasumaine Road offices of the Bangkok World, with noodle shops next door, Wat Saket Ratcha Wora Maha Wihan's temple of the Golden Mountain rising up nearby, Second World War Japanese presses out back and a jasmine beflowered spirit house out front wherein the invisible imps were given a paper to read each day. Who could plan such a thing? No one, that's who. It can't be done. It is impossible.

But it did happen. It happened steadily as if moving on iron rails, when no particular link of the passage seemed at all to leap to some wild new place but, instead, always felt to be easing exactly right and ever-normal, almost inevitably – even when there was so little in any of the steps to either predict or justify the depot at the end of the journey.

An Army officer? There was never much of an imperative in the family toward military service or, certainly, of being part of a distant war in jungles, swamps and hillsides on the other side of the planet entirely, notably a war so senselessly conceived and so unpopularly sustained. The Celtic character didn't much argue for the snappy obedience upon which the military structure is so carefully, often thoughtlessly, dependent. Editor and publisher? Surely there was never any anticipation that the small skills I had developed in classrooms and as a cub reporter for the Boston Globe, even hauled through the keyhole of military training and experience, could lead me to 24-karat newspapering in throbbing Southeast Asia, running a paper entirely when it was only something less than a decade since my principal newspaper achievement was delivering them on my bike. But so it happened, and I pinch myself still at the awesome, enrichening magic of it.

As with so much of life, there was no map, no blueprint, no foreshadowing but, instead, a jingle-jangle unfolding of wandering events so wistfully inexorable as to present the illusion that it was all being done by some clever design. But it was not, and thank the stars for that.

A hand stuck up into the air, an oath taken for little other reason of mine than that it simply seemed the right thing to do; no small reason at all, that. A beauty queen. A coin flip choice. A list to a bloody elsewhere that filled up at the fellow just before me. And there I was in Thailand. Then, loose lips at a cocktail party. The curiosity of the guy with the stars. A friendship that I hovered at the edge of. A very famous man lost in Malaysia. Jungle searches, a mind-reader's dipsy eccentricity. Sadness. Important people in league; a small, cog whirling in the innards of the effort. A bemused editor who too soon left me his cat – and his job. Incredibly, a beautiful young woman's enabling derring-do. Openness. Generosity. A challenge. Change. Dice-tossing. Criss-crossings of expectation and opportunity. By such as that, years and years ago, I found myself dizzy in the world of Bangkok, atop the Bangkok World.

It is a five-year story maybe worth sharing for the few moments, I think, before it is lost entirely to uncaring, all-devouring time.

However historic the great events of the years – Southeast Asia in the Sixties and Seventies, with its many wars and tectonic grindings of international essences against one another – there is probably little for the historians in the accounts shaped here. Good. Hopefully, it is better than lifeless that. This is no scholarly tale, suffocating life within a fog of analysis or codicils, addendums and dusty, archivist gold-panning. That is well beyond me. This is meant as no authoritative account of an era so much as reflections of a view from the era's better belfry. It is intended as story-telling as we all do with one another, and the stories are my own, not the chroniclers'. Seldom for them is there room for the light laughter there is in the bizarre or the beautiful, of quirks, of the spaces between the notes, or the children's smiles; not for us, in exchange, the indigestion of the mighty that they so much prefer to examine to death. There are few deep footprints of mine here on this history of theirs, so much as the scratches made in dashing to the side to avoid the trample of great forces shouldering aside the trees along the path. Much as ants might hope to be spared the unknowing, uncaring tread of momentous pachyderms lumbering along, so, too, did we dodge to the edges to allow the ponderous worthies their route, and filled in behind to enjoy the grander air of life itself. History only pretends to consider, I think, the unfortunates innocently or otherwise in the path of those few who commit acts of history. For the rest of us, it is life that needs to be lived while there's still time and there are our own stories to tell of what it was like.

But it was not nothing that we did and saw in Southeast Asia, in Thailand, in Bangkok, in those incredible times long ago, but only yesterday in memory. It was so alive, too. It was fascinating, important, exuberantly alive. We worked and usually laughed at the whole game.

We enjoyed a vibrant bit of life in an exotic place in an electric time. How we got there and what we did in our own bemusing way is as forceful to us as the foot-thuds of the grandees; and our stories are just as fit to be told, too, as vital as any of the weighty, multi-appendixed tomes wanly reflecting august developments rather than life's vitalities, cataloging, as they wearily do, tiered-philosophies and cast-iron principles more than reminding of the joy there is in being in life over one's head or the breath-catching awe of a newborn's grabbing of his father's finger for the first time. In Bangkok, Thailand.

Where is there space in history for that? Well, it's history's loss, although history will push forward uncaring and unknowing. History? These are stories, my stories. I cannot tell my wife Pat's story nor those of the guy sitting next to me, the ambassador at his huge desk or the taxi driver shuttling us around town. Surely their stories are as valuable, and maybe much more so, than my own but it is only mine that I can tell. Because I was there.

It is good that I am not under oath in telling this odd tale. The truth? The whole truth? Nothing but? There is truth enough in these five years of footnotes to distant events, but I cannot hope to deliver the whole truth, as that is never knowable; and I consider "nothing but the truth" to be too pale to capture the energy, color and spirit of the times and my shadowings among them. My perspective was better, I think, than that of those examining ancient things by academic squint or dull, impartial telescope; however modesty might want to aw-shucks the "me" out of memoir, these are my stories; I was along for the ride and this is what remains with me so long after.

The wondrous photography of Bill Harting, on the other gently polished hand, relays impression and reality well beyond just capturing instants of time as they passed through the glass. There is no challenging the beauty and honesty therein of selection, of tone and texture, powerful, poignant, irreducible. His grand gift of seeing the richness and capturing its message brings timeless vitality, creativity – and permanence – whose greater contribution is inspiring us to see, to recall, to imagine, to admire, to understand. I tip my hat to him, my friend.

I HAVE BEEN BACK TO THAILAND SEVERAL TIMES since the moments recalled here. Each new visit has been more so wonderful on its own, refreshingly vibrant in a culture that has changed so much but which also protects so much of that which makes it so important in the first place. Unlike many other treasures to fall victim to the leaden hand of progress, much of Bangkok's glory of old is still there right now – but sometimes shadowed over by the highrise mausoleums of its development. There are now tall office buildings everywhere, monorails and subways even. But the old quiet corners remain quiet once you pass into their hushed environs. Coming back, it is startling to see where this gentle land has traveled, but reassuring to appreciate that there is so much of the history and spirit still treasured as it has been for so many centuries. It all hasn't been paved over, one is relieved to find.

But not any one of the returning experiences, nor the accumulation of those since, can hope to rival the original. How could it? Why should it? The city has, in fact, changed. The world has assuredly changed. I certainly have changed, improved, matured. Maybe. Aged, at least. But the new me in the new Bangkok, for all of both of our vastly increased capacities, could never make what once happened happen as well once more.

Simply, too many of the pieces were uniquely of their time – some sadly so. Our wars, our military, our newspapers, our gambles, our flexibility to move about in this brilliant planet of ours create any number of odd avenues and trails to unique adventures. Yes. They even may be quite better than the adventures of those moments when it was my own turn to walk so by the walls of the Grand Palace, of Wat Phra Kaew, of Phrasumaine Road and so much more. I acknowledge them respectfully in their new force and authority. But, deeper down, I so much more appreciate the frozen-in-resin quality of what we witnessed and achieved back when the earth, as it always does, was spinning off into an especially rich new orbit – one of new energies, new understandings, new demands, new music, new freedoms, new attitudes, new worlds entirely. Those times set me on an entirely new road in life; and I am grateful for that.

AN EON AFTER THOSE HAPPY SEASONS, I have good friends still from that Bangkok world, that Bangkok World. There are people in that riverside city today who were there with us before; there are others who, too, moved far to sample other opportunities in different places and we stay connected – in what we do now and what we did together back then. Our oldest son was born in Bangkok, a better souvenir than all the statues of elephants and paintings and the million memories I carried away when it was time to leave, to come home to a land that in a brief span of awesome change and challenge of its own, had become as different and almost as alien as Southeast Asia was when we first arrived there on our amazing adventure. The spiritual links to the city are strong. The city and its society are as welcoming and as engaging now as ever before. But so different.

I arrived in Thailand a young man with barely two nickels to rub together and left half a decade later slightly older but pretty much in the same state – except that from one point to the other I was astonishingly lucky enough to have a wife, a baby son, military memories and a fascinating, incredible season navigating the seas of newspapering in a world that was hardly my own but in which I was so rewarded to have a part. The winds would carry me to wonderful places in the times since those happy Bangkok years. And it may be that the time in Thailand prepared me for little that I would confront later, diverted me, in fact, from amassing the better skills and attitudes that so benefited my contemporaries. Maybe. But I have done well enough for me and there is not a day of my life and career since that I would trade in for something different. Yet the subsequent experiences, the wild newspapering ride from Washington to New England, the pale distinctions, the books and other baubles might understandably defer just a bit to a magical time in Bangkok, Thailand, so many years ago when everything was new and dazzling and, well, fun.

Oops

IT WAS A TEST, any dope could see that. They were playing me for a fool, seeing how much they could get away with from the new guy. I had been warned enough of the edgy dealings of the crowd over at the Bangkok Post that it was hardly much of a surprise when Vonchalerm, our wily Thai general manager, stopped me in the hall and gravely told me that they were once more throwing our papers off the train. "This for us is not so very good," he said in his uneven English, an English at its worst still leagues better than my Thai.

Not good? Well, of course not.

We only sold a few thousand copies at the phantom U.S. air bases up-country but a few thousand was a lot to our Bangkok World, a newspaper whose circulation was around thirteen thousand – give or take five thousand or so. Even at the end of it I never quite knew what the circulation exactly was. But I knew enough that having several thousand newspapers thrown from the train into the damp rice paddy of some startled farmer on the iron route to Korat, Ubon and Udorn and elsewhere where the bases were was not entirely a good thing. Not such a great thing for the rice farmer, either.

This had happened before. Even as I was only new to the odd authority as editor and publisher of the Bangkok World, the oily Bangkok Post crew had already found a way to kick our bundles off the early morning, northward-bound train. I had sent a brisk message of complaint over to them, not too far around the corner actually, and heard back in the most aggrieved terms how they were just astonished and amazed that such a thing could happen and wouldn't they rather have the nails pulled from their fingerends than be in any way part of such a shoddy practice and wasn't it only just another sad sign of the contentious and troubling times we live in that such an unfortunate but likely purely accidental thing as that could take place at all, giving a bad name to all good professionals and institutions especially like that of your respectful friends and admirers over here at the Bangkok Post and we hope you are having a very nice day.

We then went to the expense, as did the Post, of having men travel with the bundles but somehow that didn't help very much as our crew always just happened to be in the other car when the papers went sailing overboard, probably spending on rice whiskey and the kerosene that passes for Thai beer the small bribe it took to ensure that they had vanished when it was time to send aflying our poor newspapers. Very annoying. So I advised my people, "Throw *their* papers off the train."

For a few days, then, the rural landscape would be littered with Bangkok Posts and Bangkok Worlds until the game grew wearying and petered out. They would start it up again some weeks later, always, it seemed, just when there was some special need for the papers to make their arrival in timely shape, just when our distributors were threatening us over our uneven service, pledging to withhold payment, to dump us. It seemed more than a coincidence. They seemed to always know when it would do the very most damage.

"They have a spy in the business office," said the always affable and wise Giorgio Berlingieri, one of the paper's owners, the "Ital" half of the gigantic "Ital-Thai" conglomerate that built roads and skyscrapers and ports and ran the majestic Oriental Hotel that bejeweled the riverside of the Chao Phrya, and in so many other ways prospered as Thailand was belatedly drawn rather reluctantly into the 20ᵗʰ Century, more than sixty years behind the times – if being "behind" such times as those were was somehow considered a bad thing. Along the line, Giorgio had been persuaded to consider it smart business to buy the newspaper, buttressing the survival prospects of the slight outfit with its American inclinations – as contrasted with the British-owned Bangkok Post – and, very possibly, thus keeping a bit on the good side of the contract-awarding U.S. embassy in the process of the game. It was a small but bright investment, although one that likely gave him more headaches than the others combined.

"They have a spy in the business office who's telling them when to hurt us the most," he said, with an operatic arch of his eyebrows and a conductor's wave of the hands at the great perfidy of it all, the dark debasement of all that is good and noble.

"That is terrible," I said. "How do we know they have a spy in our office?"

"Because my spy in their office told me," he replied. Ah.

So this time when I learned that once again their agents were jettisoning our lovely newspapers, papers we had worked so very hard to get out in complex circumstances that would baffle any modern practitioners of journalism and commerce alike, when I heard that this precious journal so rich in our spirit and sacrifice and effort was going over the side at the hands of the other guy's villains, it was in high exasperation that pointedly and with as much steel as I could deliver I once again commanded of their newspapers, "Throw them off the train."

Oops.

It hardly seems at all fair that I should be faulted for every little thing that goes astray when conflicting appreciations of the various languages of a richly international community scratch up against one another causing sparks to fly off in quite a different direction than was probably intended; it seems surely wrong to imagine blaming me that my simple instruction should be caught in a linguistic updraught to deliver quite a different conclusion than what I am almost sure I had charted for it; who could ever believe that a gentle, poetical sort such as your pal, Denis Horgan, Editor and Publisher of the Bangkok World, would at all have thought for even an instant that the "them" in the instructions to "Throw them off the train" would be construed to mean, not the Bangkok Posts, but, alas, the agents of the Bangkok Post themselves who were, in fact, hurled from the train into the rural rice paddies by our own men. My, my.

Of course, there being so little justice and understanding of life's little mishaps, a great howl went up from the Bangkok Post, assailing me to all ears as a pure madman and criminal to inflict such an outrage and wouldn't you expect just that from a misplaced cowboy, some crude American gangster cousin of Mr. Al Capone of Chicago, USA, pickled in violence and twisted in disproportion and ...

...and never again did a single copy of the Bangkok World get thrown off the early morning train on its way north, up towards Vientiane across the Mekong with connections to Korat and Ubon and Udorn and other such places, and never again did the farmers along the route sleep anything but the sleep of babes, knowing that they were free of the rain of falling newspapers.

What a world. How on earth did I ever get into this thing?

Good question.

On Time

FLYING HALFWAY AROUND THE WORLD, so many thousands and thousands of miles, with far more weary-plane stops all along the way than is now the practice unlike as it was back in a time when China was still Red and there'd be no passing through its fist-shaking space, with get-out, get-back-in-agains required in Chicago and San Francisco and Seattle and Anchorage and Tokyo and Manila, for all that hemispheric flat-pebble skipping, I arrived wrinkled from Boston into Bangkok groggy but precisely on time. All that way and not a minute early, not sixty seconds late.

On time.

Of course that perfect punctuality was something less of an accomplishment in 1966 Bangkok than it may seem. All the planes arrived on time at Don Muang Airport.

Don Muang in those days was very little the city-sized international megaport that welcomes visitors in their millions to Thailand today. Then, it was a small Casablanca-like field, bustling in its exotic fashion with international and internal flights, yes, but hardly the plane-a-second world hub it has become with hundreds of flights a-landing and a-taking off, with tens of thousands of passengers monsoon-flooding into the astonishing, arching glass palace of Suvarnabhumi International which has, in turn, relegated poor old Don Muang to nostalgia status, a sturdy secondary little strip modestly serving the country's up-country travel.

Ah, but in its day it was quite fine enough, open-airy with big ceiling fans and potted palms like a hotel lobby in the old movies, where the planes taxied to nearly nearby and the passengers took little buses in the rain to the terminal, or walked if they could bear the parboiling Southeast Asian sunshine. But no matter what – no matter the weather, the distances, the complications along the long route – they always arrived on time.

Consider: If you were to go out to the airport to meet a flight, you'd look up at the information board over the ticket desks and it would say, in plastic letters hand-set onto the chart, "PanAm flight 001 from Hong Kong, Due in 3 p.m. On Time." Excellent. How pleasant.

So you would have a seat or pace calmly around to while away the wait, idly taking in the sights of the low-grade, far-flinging excitement and pondering the certitudes of life's existence and its knotty little challenges, too, such as what might "while away" actually mean, all this as little birds would sneak a shortcut through the wide open terminal windows, the kids selling little plastic bags of sliced sugar cane, selling Coca Cola, selling dried squid that would leave the eater with breath capable of stopping a locomotive. For all the bloody frictions of the region, there was little security to slow you down, or to keep you from wandering around pretty much anywhere you pleased. People would come and go, almost always smoking, seldom confused about lines or gates as there were so few options as to where to go and come anyway. And you would wait. And wait some more.

Two or three Compari and sodas later, at 3:45 or so, and with no sight of PanAm flight 001, you'd saunter back to check the board and read, "PanAm flight 001 from Hong Kong, Due in 4:30 p.m. On Time."

The plane was always "on time" because, well, they simply changed the projected arrival if the aircraft happened to be running behind. It was like a king who is something of a bad archer having some fawning courtier dash around moving in midflight the bull's eye target in his arms to always catch the arrow. In fact, the words "On Time" were actually painted on the sign. It was permanent – and, as I came to think, a happy symbol of the easy-going ways and the lack of obsession with the persnickety rules, annoying clocks and unending, pesky details which so clutter up the doings of unfortunate other lands and different societies where the grand philosophy of "my pen rai" – it's all right, it's not important – does not rule as it does in the Kingdom of Thailand.

"On time."

I can't say that I appreciated that right off the bat, or right off the plane. After more than a day-and-a-half of being jack-knifed into a tiny seat, precisely a dozen time zones passing beneath my huge soles, just getting my legs working again was the greater challenge. It was a discomfit common with arriving after such a long, long flight, a flight of jet aircraft, to be sure, but not yet the jumbo jets – "les éléphants," as the French at first tabbed them – for travelers flying in from so many distant points of the compass to do business, to visit the ancient temples and to shop and to see the glories of the palaces and lifestyle and the vibrant life-giving Chao Phrya river, to soak at the brilliant beaches in the Gulf of Thailand and the Andaman Sea as if sand failed to meet water anywhere else quite so well, to see what remained of the city canals of this "Venice of the East," to sample the unique cuisine, the frisky nightlife. Such is what we tourists do, coming to such a happy place as this.

It was not at all what brought me there, though. No, I was a soldier, a minted officer and a gentleman, although not much of either, being an Army second lieutenant – that insignificant, contemptible, dismal, brass-barred trifle so low on the totem pole of authority as to barely clear the grass roots and to be on an eyeball-to-eyeball status with the early bird's noble breakfast. I was sent there to help in the great Vietnam war that was scorching the world. But, as it was, I arrived as a tourist.

There were actual tourists aboard my Trans World Airlines flight that winged us to amazing Bangkok in the autumn of 1966, yet they had so little in common with the tourists such as we were who sometimes flew along with them: we all uniformly young, uniformly as yet untinted by the Thai sun, uniformly short-haired men each with our uniforms packed away for the trip and arriving a little pop-eyed, wilting in the furnace feel of the perpetual Thai summer with the lovely scent of spices in the air, on assignment that supposedly did not exist, at least formally so to the customs and immigration officials who absently stamped our passports exactly as were stamped those who had arrived independently to enjoy the exotic and caressingly beautiful culture of what was only far away known by then as the land of Siam.

Most of those with Thai duty on the military orders were flown directly into huge airbases deep out in the countryside but the rest of us straggled in through Bangkok, and we came in as "tourists" because the diplomatic legerdemain of the moment was that it is tourists that we must be since we could hardly be there at all as soldiers: to hear them tell it, there were no gigantic U.S. airbases and Army encampments scattered across the land, no entire deepwater port complex taking shape in the south to bring in supplies for those non-existent bases, no caravans of bombs and boxes chugging along the newly built roadways presumably going nowhere from nowhere, no sly radio sites and eavesdropping conglomerations, no huge construction and training facilities, no accumulation of tens and tens of thousands of Americans who, frankly, you could think, did not exactly blend in.

The nimble Thais have always danced so well in international deal-ings and had deftly played one power off against another to alone in the complex region preserve their independence when all else around were falling under the miserable heel of the British or the French, the Chinese, Vietnamese or someone else. There was always someone trying to take over. Or to cast their chilling shadows on the neighbor's flowers. Thailand stands apart in the entire Asian continent for having been no one's colony or subservient, always a buffer between the com-peting thieves from Europe and elsewhere. They were diplomatically supple and subtle while others around them were sapped and scalded by hegemonists, colonialists, bullies. The Thais deserve much credit for this.

The Americans, and a few others, were fighting the perpetually feisty Vietnamese nearby and the Thais had carefully invested some of the kingdom's chips with us – but, early-on anyway, they didn't want to make a big deal of it. Who exactly it was supposed to fool is not clear, this saying that the bombers which roared out of the nearby west to pummel Vietnam, north and south, to sprinkle Laos with tiny little listening devices and great big killing devices weren't actually roaring out of Thailand but from ... from ... well, from the thin air itself, appar-ently. The Vietnamese and the Lao and the Cambodians to come and so many of the Thai and the Russians and the Brits and the French and the Chinese and just about everyone else knew exactly that there were Thai fingerprints on what was going on, but for a time, my time, the idea was that maybe if you didn't admit it you might just get away with it.

I was there to be part of this military sleight of hand, itself an important element of the larger conflict churning so bloodily across Southeast Asia. It was far from a unique assignment as millions of Americans were part of the Indochina wars over time. Millions went, most of whom weren't killed or maimed, as I guess you could say looking for some small good, besides service, to find in the thing. Too many, though, were indeed killed or maimed in a grisly game which turned such mayhem into a horrible form of art. "Too many" begins at one. And, one by one, they died. The generals and historians and distant leaders count the losses, as they probably must, in abstracts – lines on a map, dots on a chart of the taken or disappearing. But on the ground those dots were people, sons and daughters, once vibrant and whole, rich with their own dreams and pleasures. And then those dreams ended. Dots? Instead it was the dead, the mangled, the haunted. Maybe being endlessly saddened by such things, you might think that in time we would tire of seeing our children being killed in the business and art of killing the children of others. You would be wrong. Seemingly we will never pass up a chance for a war and if we're short on one being handy, we'll start a new one: this was the war of the moment; lacking it, political leaders would have found another one someplace else. It is what we do. We are seldom without a war, we peace-loving Americans. Barely a decade has spanned since Concord and Lexington, or even earlier, but that we have been fighting someone, killing someone, giving up the lives and limbs of so many of our youth for footnotes to soon-to-be-forgotten treaties, to posturing whims of politicians and leaders, themselves usually having been too distracted or sheltered or dishonest to have played the bloody game themselves.

In Southeast Asia this time around we were fighting the Vietnamese as proxies in the belly-bumping against the Soviets or Chinese, the enemies of that long moment and, because they then looked from a different angle at how economic imperatives might be crafted or how the tax code applies, we had to go off to kill them and be killed in horrid warfare where ever it could be found, or sparked. Indochina – Vietnam, Laos, Cambodia – and all around was the battlefield of the instant. I was sent there among so many others to be part of it. No one asked me what I thought.

Thailand from our point of view was uniquely there for little purpose other than to make more convenient the fighting in the Vietnams, Laos and Cambodia. It was the day's Malta: A gigantic aircraft carrier. I was sent there as a tourist since it would hardly do to have me and others registered as part of a military process that the Thai government chose not to concede existed at all. But this was all rather above the thinking of any second dinky lieutenant. If they said I was a tourist, a tourist I was. The flimflam of the thing was amusing in its way, but I knew that the system wasn't going to all this trouble to send me on a pleasure jaunt to the Land of Smiles. The "tourist" designation would vanish an inch beyond Don Muang airport. There was a war to be done.

My practical idea in all this, to the extent I had a meaningful one at all, was to hunker down, to get through it safe and sound, spend my year's assignment doing whatever they told me to do and to get out of there sound and safe. I was no John Wayne, no Rambo. In fact, though, as it was, maybe I was so much more than those who usually play the Rambos – in movies or in the halls of power – just by the small fact that I actually happened into the military service and the wars of the moment when they, of course, wouldn't have dreamed of doing anything so rather impractical as that. They, and so many like them, had better things to do than to be in the military, particularly when there were so many dumb, inconsequential others of us to go instead. I had signed on for the Army even before this latest conflict had escalated to monstrous blood-flood levels and, even as it grew like some ghastly illness, there was nothing to do but to honor the handshake when it came my time to go in. With any wondrous good luck, I would find myself in a treetop and hide from all the blistering miseries of the moment. Possibly my modest plan lacked silver-screen grandeur, the military braggadocio and diplomatic three-card-monte flair of the greater contests being played around me, but, all in all, it seemed like a pretty good idea to me. Keep my head down. As the new doctors are extolled to do, I would try to do no harm and maybe no harm would be done to me. I would cast no shadow in Southeast Asia, glide in, slide out 12 months later. Hello. Goodbye. Tellingly, the Thai word for each was the same.

As it happened and as with almost every other of my plans then, before or since, it hardly worked that way at all. Better things entirely took place instead.

WE TOURISTS ARRIVED IN BANGKOK, on time, in the late humid afternoon and collapsed in a heap in a city hotel under instruction to stay precisely there and to not get into any trouble. I did wake up after some hours that first night and sneaked out to walk alone around the nighttime neighborhood, totally amazed, enthralled by the other-earthly Asian clamor, the delightfully stinging smells, the strange energy floating around me where only I was the very odd element in the equation. Nicely, people smiled at me, and the Thai smile may very well be among the most dazzling sights on the planet. Small children, up far later than even I was comfortable being up, made what were clearly wisecracks to each other about the pale alien who lumbered around in their brisk aura and did so with the same smart-aleck tones that children deliver to what they imagine are uncomprehending adults in every precinct in the galaxy. And they laughed at each others' brashness, and I laughed with them.

Strange fruits looking like undersea creatures were for sale. Stranger delicacies, oddities that looked for all the streetside world like large insects, could be had for nearly nothing, and to wary me they were overpriced at that. Grown men and women squatted down at their stalls and tiny stoves in a way that made my knees hurt just to see. And if I caught the eye of a woman weaving strings of flowers to sell from a woven rattan tray or one turning over sizzling bits of unknowable meat on a bamboo skewer right there on the sidewalk, the woman would hold the gaze for a measured instant as her friends nearby would crack wise about this clumsy, miscolored farang, this foreigner, with happy wonderment at how such a race could continue going while looking so strange and pale-moonly as did such a sad specimen as this. And they'd laugh some more, richer than the gentle music of the temple bells in the evening breeze, a tingling of sound to make the heart fall warm and content. There, in the middle of the night, even as my poor brain fuzzed out in weariness and sensory overdose, all else was alive and brisk and noisy and wonderful.

Very early in the morning we new arrivals were collected like mail sacks, just as lines of burnt orange-clad monks padded about the dawning streets accepting gifts of the day's food from the unendingly faithful; we were hauled off in a small van, out of the great awakening city to run up the spine of central Thailand, past rice fields with huge water buffalo slowly pulling rice-paddy ploughs, or grazing, sometimes with little kids asleep on their backs, through tin-topped villages each always marked by orange-and-green roofed temples, or wats, with the saffron monks passing amid them, and with other trucks and cars and buses flying by at speeds that would make anyone less serene than those noontime-flame-colored monks gasp. I had scratched around the United States a bit and spent some small time in Ireland and thereabouts, but I had never ever seen anything like this. Every inch of the journey was fascinating as some new and exotic sight flourished by the minute: cats with their tails bent at right angles as if they had each been caught in a slamming door or under the rocking chair; oxen hitched together to pull small wagons; slight women in tight sarongs carrying bundles on their heads; men in their own sarongs flipping small nets into the small streams, fishing; ancients with betel-colored teeth and lips, looking like retired vampires; strings of children, like pearls, walking to school in white shirts, laughing and laughing some more.

There were only a few major roads in those times and we weren't much likely to get lost as we followed Route 1 straight north out of mighty Bangkok, which ended like a curtain's fall, or, better, one's rising; the paddies began immediately at the last buildings' edges. Eventually we took a sharp right at Saraburi onto Highway 2, which ultimately carried us up into the slightly higher, drier lands of the Issan plateau in Thailand's northeast.

There are those, maybe dizzied by the vast Bangkok energetic exoticism and the great charms of the country's richly colored, cooler, deep northwest, who fault Issan as some sort of backwater, dull and uninteresting. There are also people amused to hit themselves on the head with a ballpeen hammer. Thailand's northeast has its own very special beauty in a country where the plenty of beauty is parceled out at a dime a dozen, a dime a million, actually; everything is lovely and made more lovely still by a laughing people who weave flowers into soft jewelry to hang on a temple or at the threshold of home, or around a stranger's neck or wrist; where those flowers grow everywhere, in fields and yards, on the streets and, were it not for the napping little boys, probably on the buffalo's back as well; where the national smile is so sunshine bright as to warm up the hardest, cobblestone heart. The northeast has this in its own special, muted way and the spirit of the place and the strength of the people wafts it above the dusty comparisons to other parts of the nation where the beauty simply comes so easily.

Just getting off the plane at Don Muang, the sense of the place had embraced me like a beautiful fog. I had read a little on what Thailand was supposed to be like but I was not the least ready for the warm loveliness, the sharp colors, the smells and sparkle in the air, the niceness of the people. Simply, it made me feel happy. Maybe I was destined for this, courtesy of the lovely Apasra Hongsakula. Thank you, Miss Apasra.

Well, of course whatever the Miss Universe from Thailand was thinking she surely never gave me a thought at all, but it was her picture in the newspaper that landed me in her lovely neighborhood. Having volunteered for the Army as so many actually did in my day – while so many others most certainly did not – they whistled me up as my various university miscareers concluded and graciously offered me some choices where to be assigned once I was dutifully aboard. "Take your pick," they said, with the sly smile of a safecracker hearing a tumbler fall into place. This, of course, was a well known fraud not to be taken the least bit seriously since no one ever got his choice and pretty much everyone was being sent to the gravely building war in Vietnam or to Germany, a mere 20 years since the end of the great war there and where you could cool your tootsies at the Cold War with the Soviets nearby. I had no particular desire to go to either place but it was clearly understood that my desires had nothing whatever to do with any decision as to where I would serve. Indeed, just the opposite.

Idling through the newspaper the day that my "choice" was requested, I was bedazzled by a photograph of Miss Apasra (Apasra: "adorn, emblazon") who had recently become Miss Universe. I had never given Thailand a thought in my entire life, vaguely knew where it was, understood just about nothing of its history, culture or charms. But there was Miss Apasra smiling out at me from the paper and she was so extraordinarily or Ms Universally beautiful that she left me dazzled for the happy moment. (How was I to know that all the misses in Thailand look like that, and the great beauty pageant challenge there is how to be fair to the rest of the world, allowing someone else to win every once in a while?)

So, with no more thought than it takes to organize a breezy shrug, I wrote "Thailand" as my top choice, figuring that the invisible corporal somewhere who had my fate in his surely tiny hands would believe, since it was his job to assign me to the exact opposite of my choice, that in asking for toasty Southeast Asia I was clearly signaling for a brisk European berth; but maybe he would re-divine, too, that in giving me the opposite of what I requested he would be giving me what I actually wanted, but hadn't asked for, because maybe I cleverly had not asked for what I really had in mind, which might have been gay Paree for all he knew, so then maybe he would be inclined to send me to where I'd seemed to ask for, figuring that was not at all what I wanted, for why would I write "Thailand" if I actually wanted Thailand, whereby if he wrote me in for Germany then he would likely be playing into my double-reverse hands but if he, instead, typed in "Thailand" then he would be offending the core system by appearing to give someone something they actually wanted, however much the opposite might be the presumed case, leaving him in the pickle of not really wanting to send me to Germany where he was sure I wanted to go, as doing such was against the service's hoary spiritual regulations, and that any other Third World locale – Korea or Botswana or Texas – would be, in fact, a counter-choice confounded between my stated invention and my unstated intention, requiring him to seem to accede to my preference while, on the other hand, rejecting it entirely; or mostly. Or, possibly it was the exactly other way around.

Somewhere someone cut my orders sending me forthwith to Thailand instead of Germany or Texas or gay Paree, with an exasperated flair that said, "take *that*, Herr Underleutnant!" And so it was, again, that I was riding the little van up through the fascinating Thai countryside until arriving at what no one at all ever called by its official moniker, "Camp Friendship," in dusty Nakhon Ratchasima or, more simply, Korat.

I was assigned to a signal unit based deep in northeast Thailand, with facilities scattered even more remotely in a net or web, to accomplish things that I did not understand because I didn't have the vaguest idea of anything about big radios and signal systems and the sorts of things that the Signal Corps, of which I was part, was precisely and vitally expected to do. If they had put me on the Abyssinian translation desk I would have been no more out of place than being assigned to such a signal site. No one, of course, is perfect. When I signed on with the Army in college, it was at a place with a lot of engineering students who all were appropriately – and in sharp defiance of hoary Army tradition and for which heads surely rolled – assigned to the Corps of Engineers, those mighties who carved roads through the wilderness and built bases where no civilized species had ever visited before, always preferring such gnatty places over anything providing either comfort or absence of gnawing insects and sergeants. To a one, all the rest of us were defaulted to the Signal Corps. Why? No one knows why. It makes no difference why, anyway. It was the Army Way.

In the years since my days, the military has somehow come to be perceived as a brilliant force of faultless wizards and overarching efficiency, but, as good as we were, that is hardly the way the thing was back then. Sprawling all over its own feet, it was nearly a miracle that the military got through the day without even more damage to itself and those poor fools who happened into its path. I suspect we had more fun in our day but wonder how we did it.

Mostly, the slight Army training experience at the university which brought me my commission consisted of marching and drilling around in square circles and, besides mastering weapons not much used since Normandy, I learned pretty much nothing of any military value whatever; I did know to always start off marching on the left foot and it was the left foot that should hit the ground just when the drum thumped if there was a band keeping time. I had that down. And if someone brought a drum to thump on jungle patrol or the more ubiquitous office work or some other such arid assignment, I would know which foot was which. But you will be amazed to learn that there was simply no call for that once we actually were in the Army. Not once did we march or drill. Never. Certainly not in cramped radio sites in the easy wilds of northeast Thailand.

I had no idea whatever what these signal sites were supposed to do and even less about what was supposed to be my job in one of them. No one had ever mentioned such a thing to me at all, never mind instructing me on spending time in one, in a war, when things actually counted. It is a tribute to the legendary dart-toss of the military assignment system that I was so seamlessly air-mailed there, unburdened with nary a shred of worthwhile knowledge, inside a large green-gray box in the middle of noplace, surrounded by a thousand dials and switches that had something to do with tropospheric scatter, where radio signals were somehow bounced off a slat of the sky allowing for extended communications and pathways for bombers to follow to wreak their harm on Vietnam, only some 90 miles away from Thailand's Mekong River border. Something like that. A newspaper guy by modest training and limited experience sent to do that? Dared they sleep at all in Perth and Papua with such as me helping to guide warplanes that-a-way when, much more likely, they were meant to go this-a-way?

But there I went, a fresh new officer with not a second's training in tropospheric scatter or radios or anything technical or practical whatever. I could take apart an M-1 rifle but there hadn't been an M-1 rifle in use for decades. I could do the same with an M-14 but that was by now long discontinued as well. If they ever had a need for a crossbow-man up in the parapets, they could have looked me up. I had some vague guidance on using a compass which vaguely had to do, I think, with finding where north is, although what I would do with that particular knowledge was a mystery to me. North is the side of your leg the moss grows on, as I think I had learned in cub scouting, a bit of understanding probably not of much value amid the dials and switches of a signal room. Being young, though, it seemed only the slightest inconvenience to come up so short where someone else could think I might be expected to know anything about such as that, because I also knew absolutely nothing about everything else in military life, too. Or, either. It made no more sense or any less sense than anything else going on.

After about two days at the Korat base headquarters where I got the appropriate uniform to wear and briefings on how important it was to take the weekly Monday malaria pill, and how to most quickly find a place to vomit after taking the weekly Monday malaria pill, whose principal medical virtue was to make you sicker than might the malaria itself, I was sent toodling by Jeep to one of the remote radio sites.

There, deadpanning authority, I introduced myself to the sergeant who actually ran the thing, who surely was simply delighted to have me there but who was much too diffident to let it show; instead, he encouraged me to sit at a small desk over in the corner and read old copies of the National Geographic magazine and to watch out for falling lizards – the ubiquitous and cute little chameleons called chingchoks which would sneak in when some dimwitted lieutenant didn't close the door properly, and which would creep around the ceiling until the modest air conditioning rendered them sluggish and they would lose their grip and fall onto the startled head of said lieutenant reading the magazine below. In all ways I was particularly not to bother the enlisted men actually working for a living. It would be greatly appreciated if I did not talk or whistle or perform any one-man close-order drilling. If I did happen to have some views on, say, Croatian poetry or other such vital things as I had learned at the university, I should please not share them with the staff. Ever. Just stay out of the way, sir.

I could handle that. In fact, I did a pretty good job of it and comfortably imagined using my entire Army career reading magazines, becoming wise to the practices described therein about the distant bare-breasted Hottentots, and dodging raining chingchoks.

But it was not to be. It is never to be, that which seems about to be.

After only two or three magazines, they suddenly recalled me back to battalion headquarters in Korat where they needed someone to sit behind a desk in the supply wing lest the chair float off into the sky. Desks and chairs being more valuable than lieutenants, it seemed a wise decision. Except to me. This, I sensed, could be big trouble, because supply paperwork systems were something I was actually supposed to know about. I had been vaguely instructed in Army supply matters. Trouble ahead, I fretted.

After completing my dusty basic training at Fort Gordon in Georgia, a hellish place (the fort wasn't so nice, either), I was packing up to head off to my Thailand duty. But before I was to leave Georgia for civilization, a sergeant came in and pointed to me and five or so others, rather randomly I thought, and told us we had to go to New Jersey to fill vacancies in a three-week course in Army supply forms. Supply forms? What did I care about supply forms? Well, no one caring what I cared being the prevailing view, it was off to truly lovely Fort Monmouth for us, where we were reduced to petrifaction by lectures on supply forms for hour after agonizing hour as the siren song of the unapproachable nearby grand beaches and racetrack and college coeds sang to madden us, those who had for such an eternity heard only the whine of condor-sized mosquitoes and Tasmanian Devil chiggers in the iron-rasp southern summer sun. Can you even imagine how mind-grinding it is to listen to someone drone on about "prescribe load lists" and "TS-8364 catalogues" and the sly little differences between forms DA 2765-1 and DA 3161 all day long? Of course you can't. None of us learned a thing. We were not supposed to. We were there to take up space, not really to remember anything. What kind of Army might it be if everyone's echoing head was filled with knowledge and information that might actually mean something? Please. It was not like there was going to be a test. It's not that we were ever going to have to ever actually use the information, this noggin stuffing.

For most, though, that was the least of the consequences of the detour. finishing up the bogus seat-satisfier course, we were then told that some of our orders had been changed: of the six of us, five were reassigned to duty in the so-called Republic of Vietnam. Everyone but me. The selection ended with the guy ahead of me on the list. I still got to go to Thailand, my head supposedly rich with packing peanut knowledge about the forms of supply.

Of course I remembered none of it and was briefly anxious that I might be expected in Korat to do something close to what the system thought it had prepared me to do. I needn't have worried; the Army has seen second lieutenants before. Happily, there are wisely more sergeants than lieutenants and, more happily, they put me in the office with a major whose assignment seemed to be to crack his knuckles every 23 seconds and to speak incomprehensibly in Tennessean and to do not much else all day either while the enlisted folk took care of the forms, which seemed mostly to be about ordering National Geographic magazines. Or something. This was even better than the signal site. Fewer chingchoks.

Actually, though, I missed the companionable little lizards who were far more sociable than the major or the haughty sergeant, each of whom considered a second lieutenant as of little use except maybe as a door stop. Undistracted by anything approaching human or military respect, I came to admire the little scampering critters and how deftly they zipped along the ceiling, and I studied how some had fatter tail-stumps because, I learned, they could grow another tail should they happen to be snatched up by the stem by a hungry bird, a bent-tail cat or an even bigger lizard. Amazingly, they could surrender the original tail to the bird, scamper off and grow another one later. Did you know that? Neither did I. Such as that I had never been taught in all my vast education process. There must be a towering metaphor for life in the matter of tails, I thought. And thought and thought. Surely I could idle away my entire store of Army hours on such as this, do my time, and be sent home where the fairly perfect Patricia Alerding, the best and most beautiful woman in the world, remained working on our plans to be married on my return. She would undoubtedly be fascinated by my stories of lizard tails. The Army then would have me for only a few more ragtag months and then I would be free to go. Just keep your head low and, like the chingchok, be ready to jettison the tail in a pinch. Keep your yap shut.

Simple, right?

Fat chance.

THE ARMY OF THOSE DAYS was a great sprawling thing, a gigantic worldwide pulsing amoeba, far from the tidy volunteer force that followed when more modern thinking took hold about what to do with an Army in the first place – and when it was cynically determined that you could also end the youthful protest against wars by ending the draft; sure enough, the antiwar demonstrations largely would vanish when the war was left for others to do – the spark for the turnout so often not being "antiwar" but "anti-me-in-the-war." We continue in our long war-a-week tradition, but since it is some other guy doing the fighting few bother to complain, very few young people protest, few at all frivolous considerations of "peace" enter the vapid thought process from New Year's Day to New Year's Eve. Military service is sort of like Mozambique: you are instructed by the world that it's out there someplace but since you're not ever likely to go there, what do you care what it's like?

Maybe and hopefully it is a more efficient Army, if not always a better one. In the shadows of the terrible world wars, of sad old Korea and angry Vietnam, a tighter military has long since been developed, full of specialists and precision, using amazing and amazingly expensive technology. Good. Yet a far smaller volunteer force is largely untroubled by malcontents within it who do not want to be there or those with differing views coming from pages of the human atlas, maybe less inclined to do exactly and always what they are told. In so many ways, we may have a better Army even as it may lack some of the uneven cautions found in spirits around the joint that will be getting out of there soon and returning to what was invariably and tellingly called The Real World.

In those unendingly challenging earlier times and fed by the huge draft, the military counted itself in the millions and millions – and not all of those millions much wanted to be there with the others. The professionals at the top usually begrudged the inefficiencies and eggshell-in-the-mayonnaise quality of that cranky element, but I often thought it to be a good thing, the service not being populated only by those dedicated to satisfying its every whim. A problem with having a big army is that there's a tendency for someone to want to use it. The draftees and officers from sources beyond the academies, while just barely about as professional as you could get away with, could well be less likely to find unquestioning merit in the madnesses of warfare that appealed to those who sat in politicians' offices at home looking for chances to play with that gigantic military toy of theirs, uncluttered as most of them were themselves with any experience of what their wars were like to live for – and die for.

Of course there was always a huge number of people who simply didn't go in at all, at a time when all were supposed to go in. Beyond the unfit and the lucky, there were also those of stature and family, wealth and craft, guile, luck and occasionally principle, who managed to skip service entirely, leaving the dirty work to the rest who did not exist at all in their thinking anyway. Instead of joining in on the fun, they remained at home while the millions of others went into uniform; and how often it happened that those many who declined to serve would later affect the grandest faux support for those poor saps who went in their place; more than that, there were even many, spared any peril to their own limbs or lives, who worked and continue to work so hard to create even new wars as bloody in their way as the one they let others fight for them when they had that chance to go themselves. In a world of awesome technology and computers that can count the grains of a Martian sandtrap, surely it is possible to determine who it was who took the spots declined by the Dick Cheneys or Rush Limbaughs or Muhammed Alis or Newt Gingrichs or Joe Liebermans and the others – for the system did not at all come up short in its needs because people slipped past the unheeded door-knock; if the need was for one hundred men the service did not get only ninety because ten decided they wouldn't go; someone else further down the list was called upon instead. Someone went in for them. Mightn't it be interesting to know how they fared while those they replaced grabbed up the best jobs, went to the neatest parties and chased, scot-free, the young charms of the day?

Within the military services and atop every castle turret were the professionals who did, indeed, train to be there, who believed precisely in what they were told to do because it reflected their deep principles, their faith, their sense of duty and honor – or, if for no other reason than that they were told to do so by people with more authority, more stripes, more brass, more power. They genuinely took it all very seriously and pointed the sharpest sneer upon those around who did not. You can always kid yourself that someone's not being entirely a team player made much of a difference, and it goes too far to imagine that some of those lifers and ring-knockers took into understanding account the reluctances of the passers-through to help the lifers advance up the ladder by losing an arm or an existence on some foolish extra battlefield; but having some representation of the reluctant added a needed flavor to the mix. Heaven spare us all from a military where no eyebrow cranks up at some cockamamie strategy developed from on high, one that has the tin-plated merit of making its author look statistically good at the horrible expense of the folks who pay the price down below – folks who know, as we said at the time, that to be able to say that 99 percent of the bullets fired at you missed is an excellent statistic but that darn remaining pesky 1 percent takes some of the luster off the accomplishment. Don't make it easy for them, was a wise way to live – with "live" being the operative imperative.

One could hope, as I did, that in something so enormous as the United States Army it would be quite possible to slide behind the crowd's shoulders, dip under the surface, ooze back into invisibility like an eel into mud and never be quite seen again, to blend into the mass of uniformity that is the system's operative essence. Do your job but don't let it show. There was a fantastical annual officer evaluation theorem that spoke to my calculations. If someone were deemed to stand out as either very good or very bad and the point needed to be made in the annual eval, that meant extra work for the person writing the review which no one read anyway. You had to justify the particularly good grades or crisply define the failings that lead to the ranking in the other direction. Extra effort is the bane of working people. So it is, it was said, that the perfect review was simply: "This average officer is not a known Communist." Turning the essence of that inside out, one would strive to be so bland as to never cast a shadow. A nice plan and it doesn't always work, but it's certainly worth a try, I thought. Otherwise, if you're going to let being in the Army get in the way of being in the Army, why, it just takes all the fun out of it entirely.

If for some odd reason you thought it was a good idea, you could do your entire time in the Army of those days and never much discover that there was a world outside its bases and the culture within them. I never saw much of Georgia when I was sentenced there, mostly because they kept us so exhaustingly busy crawling around in the dirt and running from place to place for no purpose at all, and shooting guns and exercising for no reason whatever. There was little energy left to go out and paint the town red. As it was, there also was no town. The base was so isolated in the already red-clay wilderness that it took more time or energy than we had left to see anything. Someone once tried to tell us that the august Masters' golf tournament was played in a beautiful greensward thereabouts. Couldn't prove it by me. Greens? In Georgia? I doubted it.

In northeast Thailand, not at all dull but neither exactly the most colorful part of that blazingly brilliant kingdom, it was less the workload that kept the folks on the base so much as the fact that there wasn't all that much to see or do close by, except in the honky-tonk

world of beer joints and bar girls and other tawdry delights – delights which American officers were discouraged from sampling too
much lest they bump into there too many of the boozed-up people
with whom they were, in the morning, expected to share brilliant
reflections about articles from the National Geographic and the like.
So it was that in those early days the Thailand that many mostly got to
see was largely speaking American and it was so uniformly young and
homesick, people who had such oddly short haircuts and who drank
too often and too much.

Myself, I found the life beyond the base fascinating in that it was
simply so exotic, so different, so amazingly far from anything I'd experienced before. The city of Korat was a rough-edged enough place
on quick glance. It was a regional center for the northeast, but that
wasn't saying much. Some shops, a small vegetable market. Before the
bases came to the north, the farmers of Issan might grow enough rice
and tapioca for their own needs but there wasn't any easy way to move
along any surpluses, which could make a huge difference in a family's
income – if the middlemen weren't such thieves and bandits. It was
the home of very warm and welcoming people, of a slightly deeper hue
than those of lowerland Bangkok, folks who were just trying to make
ends meet even with the sudden and intrusive new presence of American warplanes that boomed all through the day, of hundreds of noisy
people from far away who surely spent a lot of money, yes, though not
too much of it did good for the family trying to feed itself and get the
kids an education. Slowly, though, over time, there were new jobs,
new routes and new opportunities – but it was the old ways that were
so fascinating to someone who had never seen anything quite like this
before.

On some weekends one of the Thais in the office, Khun Samarn,
would use his own free time to take me to see the local temples, mod-

est affairs compared to those of Bangkok or Chiang Mai, but impressively lovely in their own authenticity and spirit. Always he would pray, and I would feel clumsy and heavy-footed at his simple reverence. Often with his young family, we would drive around the countryside and explore the festivals or markets or just absorb what I could of the interesting nature of the land and its people there. We wandered through the old Khmer ruins of Phimai, with their distinctive beehive stupas, relics of earlier ages when forces from what became Cambodia and what was now Thailand routinely invaded each other, implanting great Ozymandian temples and palaces to demonstrate the unending power and authority of this season's victor – and which would endure as weathered relics whose importance was, centuries later, in their haunted beauty, not as any token of fleeting might. Samarn loved music of all sorts and took me to Thai nightclubs, and once or twice to the travelling open air Chinese opera, where the music had the sound of a hundred pots and pans dropped down a flight of cement steps and the singers whined like air raid sirens at the top of their lungs for an hour or so, garishly made-up, hopping around the stage in a clatter of drums and squawk of horns to the huge amusement of the tipsy crowd. And of me.

It was a great experience and I enjoyed its every second. Samarn – it is the Thai custom to refer to someone by his first name – seemed pleased at my interest, I think, and would consult with friends and family for new fascinations to share. I was honored at his kindness.

In time, I would come to know much more than that about Bangkok, merely 150 miles away by road but nearly light-years away in so many other vital measures. The great metropolis was even then no fantastic village of houses on stilts with buffalo sleeping beneath; instead, it was a huge Asian metropolis of 5 million or 8 million or 10 million, depending on whom you asked, and depending, too, on whether the huge cross-river community of Thon Buri was lumped in. It had some very tall office buildings but was most notable for its incredible Asian energy, the bustle of its streetlife existing side-by-side with serenely beautiful temples and monuments. There were a few of its once-vital canals, or klongs, still threading through the city trying to find their way to the Chao Phrya river, but mostly these had been filled in or become clotted with silt and refuse. Markets boomed everywhere, Chinese markets and vegetable markets and markets actually floating on the river where you could buy fruit or trinkets from women in tiny boats. There were whole neighborhoods of jewelry stores, others of hardware shops, still others specializing in alcohol and mischief. There was theater and culture, faith and reverence, mind-splitting noise and the softest silence. People laughed; they shouted; they called out in grand enthusiasm – and would fall totally quiet at a streetside shrine. Music was everywhere, absolutely everywhere. flowers would grow up from the cement or flow down over a wall along a busy city street like a blanket of color and fragrance. The air was thick with the spices, smells and heavy dusts of Asia and the tingling sensations of a million little stoves and grills as food was endlessly prepared in doorways, along the sidewalk, in small restaurants the size of closets in differ-ent lands. Most beautiful of all, the Thai people smiled in greeting, in punctuation, in relaxation, inexhaustibly.

Up in the country, Korat was so much more muted, more dedicated to getting through the hard day. Thailand's northeastern plateau has little of the natural wealth of the country's long core, the fertile two-rice-crops-a-year valley of the Chao Phrya river. In Issan, the weather is chalky, the land dusty and the people considerably poorer. The government did little enough to help what was surely considered an unfortunate backwater, a dry backwater at that. But the area has its own richness, its own music and dance, its own character, one found in the distinct cultural flavors moving both ways across the Mekong, which wraps Thailand's northeast quarter as border and life-flowing artery of commerce, culture and adventure, separating the kingdom from poor punching-bag Laos and the nearly inexhaustible beauty and pain of Cambodia below.

The U.S. bases scattered across the region provided rare new opportunities for work, pumping money into a region that had seen little of it. The long roads we built to service the bases contribute enormously to the region's improvement as it suddenly became possible for farmers to get supplies and news more easily, to work around the heavy-handed government officials and middlemen who bilked the farmers at every turn, to ship additional crops for cash than was possible before. It is a very special place, Thailand's northeast, and that it seized the heart of a city kid from Boston so thoroughly is a great gift it hardly knew it was giving.

The Army base, Camp Friendship in the lingo of some poetry-addled knickname-maker who surely had never set a foot in Korat, Thailand, was an orderly cluster of small barracks, offices and depots. There were chapels and clubs, used in rather different frequency, a few basketball courts and that's about it. Guarded by American and Thai military police, the base was safe and comfortable. The gigantic air base next door roared with its own iron energy and housed movie theaters and a big PX and many creature comforts scorned as unnecessary luxuries for us by the Army planners who were themselves basking by the distant Hawaiian beaches, who made the decisions as to what the trifling dust-covered soldiers far away should experience. I figured that was fine with me, anticipating that the less anyone thought about the otherwise invisible denizens of Korat, the better off we'd likely remain. I imagined that I would be able to move along in the shadows until it was time to scram.

THEN BRIGADIER GENERAL EDWIN FAHEY BLACK arrived on the scene and, more than ever, it was time to buckle the seatbelts: My ride was about to get wondrously bumpy.

We weren't worth a general before, existing as a multi-use battalion and then as a logistical command, whatever that is. But we could hardly be trusted to make a mess of things on our own without a general of our own as things got larger and larger. As a general thing, so to speak, generals are to be best avoided. The upgrade that compels such rank-firepower has a nasty tendency to call out for being put to use where, before, we could slink to the side as great events boomed around us. For most military people, generals are up there in the thin clouds, acknowledged but largely ignored by folks with actual work to do. With luck you would never run into one. (During the soon-to-follow Watergate years, an Illinois representative, Bill Hundley, would pop Republican smugness as they tried to distance themselves from their Richard Nixon and wrap themselves in the aura of Dwight David Eisenhower, Eisenhower, Eisenhower. "Hey, I knew Ike," Hundley would say. "We were in the Army together." Anyone with military time would get the cheeky preposterousness of that.) With any skill you could go your whole life and never have anything to do with a general. That would have been fine with me, too, enjoying the generals from a true distance such as you might enjoy a tiger in a zoo or a great white shark on the movie screen.

It didn't work.

After General Black arrived and settled in, they held a command performance reception at the officers' club and we all shuffled in and headed immediately for the bar. No one in his right mind was looking to make small talk with the new general because, well, he was a general after all, and the early word was that he was very tough and

demanding and particularly hard on emptyheads, a commodity found
in some abundance in Camp Friendship. Lieutenants, meantime,
were beneath coffee-grounds in the scheme of things and most of us
admired that uncluttered level of status. The general was just in from
another tour with an infantry division in Vietnam and took this whole
war business very seriously. Avoid him, was the advice that made
the rounds. Head for the bar instead. Then again, the bar is what we
always headed for at any gathering of people short of church service,
which itself only delayed the bar for its 45 minutes. As always, at the
party lieutenants formed up British squares with other lieutenants.
Captains clustered with captains. Majors and colonels stuck together,
too. Such was called mingling.

Well, as my luck would have it, just as I slithered around the edges
of the military rub-a-dub, of course, what luminary do I squarely
bump smack into but the general himself who, I think, was slithering in the opposite direction, counter-clockwise, trying just as hard
to avoid such as me and the fawning colonels and mindless small talk
of such events. There was no escape. I had been looking for the exit,
figuring that I had made quite enough of any impression as I was likely
to accomplish just by being there, and it was wise to scram. Being
seen once was plenty enough and little good could come of anything
more than that. I had sort of mastered the being seen/disappearing
act in the beginnings of my newspapering life when, as a copy boy at
the Boston Globe, they wildly expected me to show up at 7 a.m. some
days. Seven a.m.! Can you imagine? I certainly could not. I discovered that the bosses, of course, were not there at that horrid hour, so
the day before I would put an old jacket over my chairback, spread out
papers as if I were actually hard at work but had just stepped aside
on some vital errand – and I would saunter in appropriately later, at
9 a.m., like the Magi in reverse, by a different way, leaving my actual

jacket in a closet along the route, showing up as if I had been there for hours. They never tumbled to it, and I figured on pulling off the same on the brass at the bosses' toot: arrive with a flourish, then slide out the back door. But, mid-slide, there was General Black. I was trapped, while he likely felt that he was the one trapped at having to conjure pleasantries for a mere lieutenant.

We made the most idle of small talk, me answering his light questions about who I was and where I was from and what I could ever possibly have done of any interest, even while I tactfully declined to pose those self-same questions to him, cleverly suspecting that we weren't exactly on the same level of chums to be equally probing of one another. In time, I did manage to wriggle free and to blend back into the crowd and out the door before making too huge a fool of myself. Good job by me.

But the next day the word was around that Black had the dragnet out for the lieutenant who used to be a newspaper guy. I didn't know it then but his wife, the nifty Cobey Black, was a noted journalist in Hawaii, and the slight newspaper link had nettle-snagged his interest in the otherwise excruciating boredom of the moment. He didn't remember my name – although, frankly, I remembered *his* – and he was looking around to find me. There are only so many places to hide on a small Army base, and hide I tried. It was understood that he tended to grind up those around him, notably young officers who were considered as toothpicks. It was certainly not at all my idea for Army life to have to do any real work, and I sensed the deep trouble in this ominous development. Sure enough, as much as I hunkered down to near-invisibility, someone ratted me out and I was called into the general's company once more, and was abruptly assigned duty as his aide. If I had been slinking in the opposite arc, I might have never run into him, but it was another of the amazing links that lead me not so much later to the Bangkok World, although there was no knowing it then.

Running with the general. So much for learning about ancient French cave paintings or the fishing habits of the polar bear from the National Geographic. So much for lizard watching. I was actually expected to start the day before 6 a.m.! Be still my heart. That we worked deep into the night was no problem, but it was simply outrageous beginning things before the Thai roosters were even up, up before the Air Force Phantoms and 105's and Wild Weasels at the handy base next door which would explode out on their morning runs for Vietnam, shaking the fillings from all nearby teeth as their afterburners kicked in over the Army base below. What kind of outfit was this? Six a.m.? If I had known at all who was my congressman I might have written in complaint but, as it was, I kept quiet and plodded the early a.m. hours like a zombie.

Hauled into heavier duty and rattling around as befuddled Robin to the general's Batman left little time for improving my mind with reading magazines or watching Chinese opera. Tough, demanding, unforgiving of the careless, hard-charging, wonderfully square, unrelentingly curious, rigid in matters military and political but endlessly fascinated by life around him, Ed Black was great fun to work for, if you had nothing else whatever to do in life except work for him.

OTHERS FOUND HIM TO BE A BEAR and he had already gone through a series of aides and assistants in his early weeks in Thailand. Much higher ranking staff officers found themselves dumped to more meaningless assignments, too, for performance below his standards. The guy was serious. Like so many of his military generation, he was in his third huge war in two decades and, also like so many of his commitment, he was totally baffled by the idea that there would be people challenging the rightness of the wars for which so many of his world were dedicated – and were being lost. It was the job, that's all. You did it. Mostly, you didn't have to question when the answers were already provided from elsewhere up the ladder. We hit it off well, though, and remained friends for many years after. He took me far from my ching-chok census as the expanding, engorging war in Vietnam and beyond swallowed up more and more of everything.

For all his vast age, certainly suggesting that dilapidation should come with such dotage – he was 51 when we first met and it was all I could do to keep from taking his ancient elbow as we walked along – Ed Black was annoyingly energetic and distressingly physically fit. He was on the go all the time and for all my exhortations that he should slow down and husband his waning powers, and lest he kill me by exhaustion first, nothing would do but he and I would be rocketing around to the various sites and locales in his command – and then some. He did exercises even when no one was looking. He ran. He parachuted out of perfectly good airplanes just for the fun of it. Up well before dawn, we'd be off by Jeep or small plane or helicopter to one corner of Thailand or the next. Or beyond.

The Army's game in Thailand was complex. There were roads being built. Supplies were being moved to the big airfields, facilities and training was at work for the Thai forces heading to Vietnam; there were the signal sites, a huge port being built at Sattahip in the southeast, a gigantic airfield under construction for the B-52s which, until then, flew all the way from Guam to idly kick their bombs out the door onto Vietnam far below and then head on back to Guam for supper. There were conferences and councils to attend. Projects to supervise. Briefing after briefing – from squads in the hills to huge formal affairs with the Thai and American poobahs. The war by now was gigantically huge and becoming more huge all the time, and the needs from Thailand growing apace. Pretty busy folks, for tourists.

At the end of the day we'd usually loll around and talk for hours more. The general would sit and jabber with the colonels about military matters, and when they were gone he and I would sit and talk about them. He wanted to know about everything, about the thinking of the troops, about the "hootches" we lived in – wooden-braced tents Croesus-rich with mosquitoes and lizards. He quickly ordered those taken down and more comfortable, fitting quarters built, and if the suggested permanency of the new facilities for his people offended anyone's vision of us not being there, give him a call. No one did. He would huff and puff about the lamebrains around him, confident that I wouldn't be lamebrained enough to go around blabbing about it. He would read the Bangkok newspapers that came in, looking for clues about what the Thai officials and others were thinking and we would discuss the news of the day. His politics were not my politics but we heard each other out, me hearing him out a lot more than he heard me out. He talked so warmly often about his handsome family, the spark of his spirit. He drank a single martini a night, loved peach ice cream when we could get it. For my wise part, I drank nothing, knowing my yacky Celtic chromosomes would betray me when tickled up by the firewater. He was a very good man, intelligent, honest, loving of the nation and its values which he genuinely believed were worth the hard price to sustain. He was kind to me, except for the lunatic matter of the 6 a.m. starts. I was proud that he seemed to like me, in his amused fashion.

This was his life, the Army, and it was not mine. I was, indeed, a passing-through tourist, fulfilling to my honorable best what I had agreed to do but looking forward to the instant that I would be a free man once more. I was not at all reckless enough to snap my fingers under the nose of authority but found it hard to take seriously every single instance of the military's stilted etiquette and its pecking order, which is to say, peck-on-those-below. Ed Black had seen such as me before and he seemed tightly amused at the loosey-goosey nature of my Army game-playing in a world of careerists. So long as I didn't dare spring any of that on him, he was fine with it. Not bad for an old guy.

Every few weeks we'd go to Vietnam to confer with the planners there, to check up on things we were supporting, to visit places where he'd served and would return to serve again later. As often as we could arrange it, we would drop in on units there, chat up the soldiers, hale and harmed alike; but so often it was just meeting after meeting. As with most institutions, if more of the time dedicated to meeting about doing things was applied to the actual doing of the things, maybe more would finally get done. If that's actually a good thing; maybe just talking about things has its own merit when, unlike as with most institutions, the consequences of daily military activity are so often measured in corpses. But they certainly knew how to do grand meetings in Vietnam. Small wonder that touring politicians would wake up only later to realize they'd been "brainwashed," in the famous career-killing characterization of presidential candidate George Romney. With amazing graphics, two-star generals would brief three-star generals using wondrous electronic tallies of enemy lives supposedly taken, inches of territory held for whole minutes and minutes at a time. Maps and billboards glistened, and if the war was fought on them instead of on the actual ground it would have been a grand triumph.

While the generals rubbed together their great heads – most often a fearsome prospect – afterwards I would drift along with other junior officers to sample Saigon's razory nightlife which, for all the French influence, was more Tijuana than Tuileries or, more likely, just shoot the breeze about the war. Over time, the shot-breeze so strongly confirmed what many people already knew: this thing could never go well. There was a real affection for the Vietnamese people but a bone-deep contempt for the Vietnamese leadership, its unending corruption, arrogance, vanity and lack of valor, its contentment to let someone else do the dying for its own protection and, vitally, its almost entire estrangement from the actual Vietnamese people. You heard it everywhere, everywhere except in the councils of the mighty where the especial interest was in using our own might to chase after the vanishing shadows of the enemy, almost irrespective of the emptiness of the ally in whose name we were fighting, in whose interests our kids were dying. It wasn't their job, our job, to perfect the Vietnamese political system; the job was to defeat those we found to be its opposition, and whom we adopted as our own enemies. It was a serious game. Deadly serious. Yet beyond those at the top, I never met anyone who thought things were going well or that the Vietnamese political leaders were even distantly worth the dime. Not one.

Gingerly over time I would talk a little with the general about such things, but his tremendous lodestar of duty, honor and service overawed what one might have guessed would be within the power of an intelligent man to see clearly. But that ignores a different truth: As were so many others, Ed Black was a professional doing what he believed was the right thing. He made no policy of war, this soldier who had been told to carry out war in Europe and across Asia almost all of his adult life. He was no politician or diplomat. He was an Army officer doing what he was instructed and what he believed to be what was expected of him. It would be so unforgivably smug for me to imagine there is any uplifting rightness to having seen things differently, more correctly as it sadly turned out. My small, shriveled soul may well sizzle to this very day in white heat at the political leaders who dishonestly sent so many out to die for nothing whatever, but that withered little spirit is buoyed and revived in respecting the bravery, honor and commitment with which those horrible rotted-out policies were carried forward.

THE SEVEN BIG U.S. AIR BASES IN THAILAND were there to pummel the Vietnamese in the north and their allies wherever they could be found; over time, eighty percent of the strikes against North Vietnam came from the Land of Smiles. In the relentless mathematics of the air war, to deliver a bomb from an F105 fighter-bomber in Korat required, of course, a Korat and an F105 and a bomb. Built the way war planes are, flying rocks, they pretty much could carry merely enough fuel to get off the ground so had to meet up with refueling KC-135 aircraft, floating gas stations, along the way, and on the route home. These would be flying from another base entirely at U-Tapao. Of course, they would require fighter cover from several other bases, reconnaissance information from planes from even another airfield at Takhli, plus a further facility with aircraft ready to help rescue downed pilots along the way, and another mile-long horizontal launching pad for the gigantic B52 bombers which would flatten their targets with pinpoint accuracy so long as the pinpoint was the size of, say, Rhode Island. And then, while the fighters were fending off and shooting down the Soviet-built jets flown by pilots who often just happened to speak Russian, there was a need for aircraft to attack the anti-aircraft missile sites so that the B52s and other warplanes wouldn't themselves be defenseless and then there was need for damage assessment flights from ... and so, on and on.

Soon enough that F105 bomb delivery required a whole fleet of aircraft and military base after military base to help it get dropped. And the bomb itself had to be transported to the airfield along routes from a port, both of which needed to be built and maintained, and the bases had to have ground security and food and paper-pushers and blankets and whiskey and planks of wood with which to construct barracks and PXs and mess halls and infirmaries. Soon enough, again, the U.S. presence in Thailand approached 40,000. It is only a little too much to say that the gigantic U.S. war machine seemed oddly gargantuan applied in pursuit of guys who wandered around almost freely where they wanted with a rifle, a few bullets and a sleeve of rice. But that's the way it's done, then and now.

The bases, not incidentally, were also there to help me make a bundle.

For convenience and common sense, the larger of our whittled-out Army encampments were often found near to these Gotham-like air bases even as we preferred to think their bases were, instead, found near to us. An Air Force base is like a small American city with thousands of people and, because they were the Air Force, they were a cheery bunch with lots less attendance to the odd rigors of military order and the obedient life that the other branches seemed to imagine is needed in stern abundance in order to function. Archly professional, the snappiness of flyboy salutes or the excruciating niceties of rank and grade there seemed considerably more casual than what was expected from the dirt eaters nearby. In trade, they had enormous base exchanges or shopping centers and five-star officers' and enlisted men's clubs. And great food, although no one tops the Navy for excellent eating. Good for them.

Another thing they also had were enormous radios sweeping the heavens and picking up programming from anywhere on the planet – and these helped finance my life as a junior officer having to make high ends meet with a scrawny pay packet each month. I got around that by insider trading, at least for a grand time in the season of the "Impossible Dream."

The Boston Red Sox were my main addiction in those days – and all days since. There are no 12-Step programs for that, brothers and sisters, and it is just as well. No one would go. We enjoyed our few vices and were in no hurry to give them up. Other obsessions would come and go but it was the Red Sox that enduringly kept me humble, deflating me against giddiness whenever things seemed to be going pleasantly. Raised in the Church of the BoSox, I brought to the great game the gloomy faithfulness that others apply to their religions, philosophies, heritages and political parties. One did not question or much examine such compulsion: it was your world-preparing burden and your anchor to heavy handed reality. Red Sox people knew that we would always lose, forever be deflated and laid low – but none abandoned the ship in favor of, say, the easy road, silver platter Yankees with their despicable sense of success entitlement and bitter operatic dismay when they do not win every season, every trophy, every contest, every at-bat. Not for us of those days the silly expectations of victory which others might entertain. Expectation? We didn't entertain even the faintest hope. Are you kidding? We were wiser than that. While those others might start the festivities imagining the manner of triumph, we began with the certainty that sooner or later the game would be blown. Cruel experience had counseled us to the madness of high dreams. The Red Sox would lose. Always. It was what they did best. There was little true disappointment when there were no fantasies to fall flat. We were tougher for that.

The early decades of my suffering were the usual dismal times for the Red Sox and their fans and we wallowed in our misery. They lost and they lost often and badly. They lost in the most imaginative ways, handing back victory as if it were too fetid and maggoty to imagine keeping. Win? Any fool could win. It took a special brand of fools to lose. That was the way it was and if you were to enjoy the Red Sox game, it was best to enjoy the game of baseball itself because your team would let you down sooner or later. My father took me to baseball games at Fenway Park in an ancient time when you could get tickets easily and they did not cost what a small automobile costs. Almost always the Red Sox lost, but what I remember to this instant, instead, are the peanuts and hot dogs, the being seated on a window sill while my father had a beer at the bar of the Short Stop saloon before the game and after. In my teenage years, I went to a million games because the kid across the street had free tickets. His poor dad had been killed in Korea and he had an uncle who took the family under his wing. The uncle worked for the Red Sox front office and so we had tickets to any games we wanted. We wanted them all. It was such great fun to go to the park, join the few thousand other jobless people who might be there and bask in the easiness of watching a great game unfold in the summer sun with no great financial or emotional investment. If the Red Sox almost always lost, well, that was what life deals.

Until the "Impossible Dream."

Famously, in 1967, after yet another cobwebbed season in baseball's cellars, the Red Sox mysteriously came to life. And started winning. They actually beat people. They even did not alwaysalwaysalways hand away certain leads as they had since Harry Frazee's day. And suddenly the fans returned and interest mounted and life was a grand thing. Even on the other side of the world. Being 12 hours ahead of Boston time, or Boston being 12 hours behind us in Thailand, take your pick, day games were being played at night – and so many of the games were day games in those balmy days, or nights. Of course, the military was not about to have numbers of its troops staying up at night – there was a war going on, after all – so they taped the games and broadcast them on Armed Forces Radio during the local "day." Fair and logical enough.

No, not fair enough.

I wanted to know who won right *now*, since there was suddenly a chance that the 'who" might actually be the Bostons. What kind of an addict is he who says, "Oh, I think I will wait 12 hours to have my drink?" That's what sherry-sippers do.

So it was that I would set my little alarm clock and wake up at ungodly hours and borrow a bicycle or, rarely, a Jeep, if there was one sitting idle, to glide through the deep, deep Thai darkness to the air base where I knew a guy who worked overnights – and who had access to the great radio system whereby the nation's military air fleet would set out to hammer Vietnam, Laos and anyone else it felt like bombing. A co-parishioner, he would let me in and we would listen to the game for a while and we had a great time of it. Then I would find my way back to my own base for a few hours' sleep. None of that delayed gratification baloney for me.

Of course, if I were to be going to all that trouble, who could fault me for making it worth my time, too? This is still America, isn't it?

So, many mornings I would groggily join my fellow officers for breakfast at the small mess hall. Somehow there were many Detroit Tigers' fans among the engineers, and the Tigers were in contention as the amazingly exciting season wound forward. So we talked baseball. We argued about baseball. We bet on baseball.

And I made a mint.

I would bet on the Red Sox in games that I knew they had already won. I would not bet on the Red Sox in games that I knew they had lost . Well, I did occasionally, just to lose a little and not make the engineers too suspicious. I would give odds. I would bet on a spread we would devise. To keep the dimbulb Tiger people from catching on, I would sometimes take bad bets they would almost force on me; but, as luck had it, the Red Sox mostly won. So I would make crazy bets – "I think Yaz will hit five homers today" or "Lonborg will strike out 21 today" – and there was so much attention to the madness of thos zany predictions and the losses I sustained on that one wild bet that they never much noticed that the four or five game bets I made always quietly won on the sly. I hated to see the season end.

Even as the military season, for its own part, might well have played along in its mad pursuit of unending extra innings, my own plan remained true, general or no general, and the star I sailed by was fixed: finish the year. Go home. Neat plan.

Enter Jim Thompson.

Or, actually, exit Jim Thompson.

Where's Jim?

JAMES HARRISON WILSON THOMPSON was indisputably a giant in Thailand and far beyond: a business mogul, a humanitarian, a social lion, an adventurer, an architect, an art collector, a grand storyteller, noted host, friend to so many. You could suspect that someone with inside names like "Wilson" and "Harrison" rather than, say, "Spike" or Sluggo," would be doing well. It was in the cards. He lived an amazing life that took one odd, wonderful turn after another and then rather suddenly blinked into mystery and darkness. Incidentally and peripherally, his mystery changed my own life, too.

Jim Thompson and the general were old pals from the Second World War days, otherwise there was little chance whatever that his path and mine might intersect creating for me a new and broad avenue entirely.

General Black and I would go to Bangkok every few weeks where he would confer with the military and diplomatic panjandrums there. I would tag along to tend to variously irrelevant lieutenant things. There, we usually stayed at Jim Thompson's famous home, an astonishing amalgam of several venerable Thai-style teak houses hauled together in simple but historical splendor, filled with wondrous art and treasures of Southeast Asian history that he had amassed in his twenty years in Bangkok. It was no museum at all then but a lovely home, a showpiece of the man's wide interests and accomplishments. It reflected the culture of the region, and of its noted owner.

During the Second World War, Thompson had been working with the various undergrounds in India and Burma, and had been slid into Thailand to help affect more warrior mischief there where the Japanese sustained an uneasy occupation over the overwhelmed Thais. He worked with the Seri Thai or Free Thai movement helping coordinate their training, their strategies and tactics. At that time and later he became close to men who would hold key positions of leadership in the postwar era, often to their sad end as other military forces shouldered them aside, dealing out pain and blood in the process. Late in the war, Jim had orders to go off to someplace in China, but when the atomic bombs were dropped he knew the war was over and hunkered down in Bangkok, ready for the inevitable endgame and the unknowable to come.

He stayed on in Thailand, always a welcoming and achingly beautiful place to be and especially so in those days, as one of the few westerners of real moment in the afterwar confusion. As so often happens, people come to nostalgically consider that a season of the past has to be so much more beautiful or relevant or amazing than this moment's, and reflections are always rich with the, "Ah, you should have known it back then ..." People tell me now how they envy my era of being in Thailand but people in my own era so often told us how much better it was long before. It is the inverse of the familiar geezer reflection, "Ah, but when I was your age we had to work 27 hours a day in the fields and walk 11 miles through the snow uphill to school ..." while their own more ancient parents would say, "Hah! He had the life of a Rockefeller. Why, when we were his age, we had to work 35 hours a day in the foundry and trek 18 miles through the hurricanes and ..." But it was likely all quite true that the days when Jim Thompson and others settled into Bangkok were, in fact, a most magical time: most things were so much simpler, all was less spoiled by the grinding of the modern moment. Memories play tricks, but sometime they are quite on the money. Jim was smitten. Bangkok was beautiful and exotic and inviting and he decided to stay. His posh old world of upper-scale Delaware was always there awaiting his return but he wanted to see what he could see of this lovely place. What he saw, he loved.

After some murky efforts of helping move the post-Japanese situation along from his espionage and diplomatic backgrounds, Jim Thompson soon relaxed into a life of the ease available to man of some presence, some wealth, someone of considerable knowledge of Asian affairs and culture, and of very high intelligence and perception. Not at all incidentally, he became fascinated with the quality and loveliness of Thai silk.

Thai weavers had long been known in Asia for the astonishing textures and colors of their silk but it was an art form that was sadly fading away, with broad cultural and economic consequences. The individual weavers usually lived far out in the countryside and received too little money from the rapacious middlemen. They were giving up their art, and, with the withdrawal of their skills and knowledge, the very presence of Thai silk itself became endangered. In a world of changing tastes and opportunities, ancient techniques were not being passed along and the gift of Thai silk looked to be disappearing into the fog of lesser fabrics and duller tastes. But Jim, whose own family wealth was itself based in fabrics, was so taken with the magical Thai silk that he moved to see what could be done to revitalize the industry.

He invested in the weavers, guaranteeing them a steady income beyond even what the silk was actually selling for in those early days. He worked to modernize techniques and distribution systems. He dedicated his own skills and contacts into promoting the beauty and exotic nature of the fabric to a world coming out of the rough grays of decades of depression and war. He sent silk to his friends in the United States, fascinating fashion leaders with its beauty. With that, and its dazzling use in the play and movie, "The King and I," – a bit of spirited musical drama that the Thais to this day loathe, portraying as it does their beloved historical king as something of a prancing cartoonish character, somehow subservient to a know-it-all British governess – the silk took off, the industry was revitalized and it made Jim Thompson very famous, very important and very rich.

Jim Thompson's house, which gradually filled with artwork from around Southeast Asia, collected and rescued in his travels, became a center for visiting grandees and a rich array of his local friends. He entertained nearly every night, pleasant gatherings of big shots and simply interesting people that Jim invited along, dining on food largely brought in from street vendors, drinking modest amounts of good wine, and discussing and arguing about all the high events of the day: the arts, high commerce, Thai politics and gossip, the sensational murder of the American editor of the Bangkok World some months before, changes in the society around them, so often for the worse, the comings and going of the expatriates and Thais of note. Often, and increasingly, it was about the war.

Staying at Jim Thompson's house, where I was forever terrified that my big feet would topple over some priceless vase or bring down the terraced treasures along the walls, possibly shattering a revered Buddha head from back when there was no America at all and when Europeans were still living in mud huts and howling at the moon, General Black and I attended many of those dinners, but it was the gentle talk-around afterwards, when the others had gone, that was the most fascinating. Black and Thompson were very good friends and they amiably danced around one another on the matter of Vietnam that was savaging Indochina, and threatening to swamp Thailand, too. Jim saw that the long poisonous war, won or lost, would change the region irreparably, polluting the soft graciousness he loved most about the place; the general felt that a Communist victory would destroy everything that Jim loved so much in any event, and that the costs to the Southeast Asians would be too terribly high. The passions of the issue were brisk, but among these two, so far as I ever saw, it was all respectful and wise.

The general liked Thompson too much to bristle overmuch at his views and Thompson clearly liked and admired Black enough to not press hard his point that the war would likely do more harm than any possible good. They were old friends.

I sat at the edges, muting my own views on the war's harsh path, and mostly just listening in and sagely agreeing with whoever was talking at the time. Jim was tickled by this and would slightly bait me into the game, but carefully without risking my junior neck with the general – with whom I would be around when Thompson wasn't there to deflect the brigadier's cold eye should he turn on what he believed to be my foolish lack of worldliness and military sophistication. The general never did, not even once, but the capacity was always there and Jim was kind enough to divert it.

Jim Thompson was a good man, and everyone knew that. As with nearly every expatriate south of the Laptev Sea, he was often seen as having richly residual relations with the American intelligence services – with which he surely did have his enduring contacts but which, by then, had moved well on to their own slightly less genteel sources for information and mayhem. Later, so much would be claimed as a certainty of Thompson's critical role as an intelligence operative, and what trouble that might have inspired for him but I never much bought into that; there was a younger and different crowd sailing that ship by then. From our own military piece of the local spooking game, I had a pretty small but pretty good guess of how it was playing, and maybe who were some of the keenest players.

What I knew for absolute sure was that Jim Thompson was kind to me, arranging with a jeweler friend of his to work up the wedding rings for my marriage set for some months down the road; he gave us a large bolt of elegant white Thai silk for the wedding gown, silk which we have until this day as the gown was already made and we were quite unable to imagine what else to do with such otherworldly material. Jim visited some with the general in the northeast on a trip to his weavers and we tried in our clumsy way to return the hospitality he offered us so generously. He was fascinating, wise, funny.

And then he was gone.

He was there one moment and quite missing the next.

THOMPSON AND SEVERAL FRIENDS had gone to the Cameron Highlands in northern Malaysia for Easter weekend in 1967. People did that sort of thing. It was a remote but wonderfully comfortable cluster of cottages in an old British hill station surrounded by high mountain jungles and awash in bright flowers, cool crisp air and, for anyone from the scratchy din of faraway Bangkok, blessedly quiet. Jim and his party relaxed away their time in the most pleasant fashion: walking, dozing, talking. On the afternoon of March 26th most of the group decided to take a nap. Jim remained outside the bungalow, where he was last seen comfortable on a lounge chair on the verandah reading a book. Last seen because he has never been seen since. Not hide or hair of him, as they say. He vanished. Without the smallest clue as to what happened to him. Gone.

We were up-country in Thailand when the general got the word that his friend had disappeared. "I'm going down there," he said to me instantly. "You want to come? We'll be on our own." Did I want to come? Of course I did. Grabbing up some clothes, some supplies and a few radios, we were off. The general whistled up an airplane and, after a brief stop to get the latest news in Bangkok and to pick up another old friend of Jim's, Dean Frasche, we rushed to Malaysia. Likely, we rushed off a little too quickly as it certainly didn't do General Black's standing any good that we rattled off into someone else's mystery like that; we never quite cleared it with the Malaysians either who affected some posturing outrage that an American military plane just dropped into its territory without permission or approval. But rattle we did.

We got to the Cameron Highlands early the next morning and did what we could to assist in the search. The story had immediately become electric as Jim Thompson was so famous that his disappearance was a huge event. There was worldwide interest in the vanishing of one who was surely among the most prominent American civilians in Asia. Henry Cabot Lodge, the Massachusetts Brahmin U.S. ambassador in Vietnam, demanded daily reports of his missing pal's status. Jim's friends in Asia followed the case's every small development; his influential family in the United States pushed for news and action. We tried to help.

The local news guys who swarmed to the Cameron Highlands and cluttered up the remote scene imagined that Black and I were there with razzle dazzle American space age technology to discover Jim's presence - or remains. They wrote that the military radios I carried were actually secret radar devices capable of penetrating the thick vines and foliage. They didn't write that they were only radios which didn't even work in the Cameron Highlands, and I lugged them around like small anvils. We prowled the jungles and knotty undergrowth with the local police and military for a few days to no little good as there was no clue to be found about what had happened to James Harrison Wilson Thompson, to Jim Thompson.

There were so many theories. He had wandered off into the jungle and fallen into a pit. He had been taken by some of the mountain tigers or other such beasts as prowled there. He had been kidnapped by ransom-seeking bandits. He had simply gotten lost. He had been spirited off as part of some bizarre political-diplomatic-espionage hoo-ha connected to the war in Vietnam. He had been killed by business rivals, social rivals, spying rivals, art collecting rivals. He had joined a tribe of native women and was living in the wilderness like a sultan with his primitive and adoring harem. He had simply thrown in the towel and walked away from it all, to his death in the wilderness. Sensationalism hating a vacuum, everything became so swellingly exaggerated: his wealth approached Carnegie status; his importance to the region's spies was such that no plot could exist without him; his triumphant work in the world of creating silk or art collecting somehow was seen to inspire a jealous rage of homicidal result, exported to far quarters of another land entirely; his disappointment in the Indochina war bloated up to where he was somehow cast as Abbie Hoffman, Jane Fonda and Martin Luther King Jr. rolled together. Supporting evidence was not much required and contradicting facts were rejected out of hand as plodding and unimaginative.

Beyond the diplomatic hoo-ha and the wilderness sultanate possibilities, there was almost something to support any theory that one favored. And something equally compelling to debunk it. It was very easy to get lost in the creepiness of the mountain jungle of the Cameron Highlands – not the clingy haunted nightmares of the lowlands and Vietnam, where ghosts and ghouls take their vacations, but thick and ropey nonetheless; but one would need to work at it with especial ignorance to start off into the chillingly embracing growth in the first place. Thompson wasn't that dumb. There actually were tigers and creatures up there capable of attacking and carrying off a grown man; but there was no blood and gore, no bits of clothing, no new tracks to be found by the experts who knew how to look for such things as that.

And, yes, there certainly were bandits active in the region, and kidnappings did occur, mostly of wealthy Chinese holidayers from Singapore or Kuala Lumpur who were quietly released later for huge ransoms; but no ransom was ever asked for from an underworld that always preferred to work in the quiet, no information pointing to even a dead body's burial was ever given despite the huge rewards offered for even his remains. Trackers found no evidence of pits or places where a man might be lost, no birds or scavengers were seen later attending to the unfortunate remnants of a frail 61-year-old man who might have died helpless in the brush. It was a great mystery and is still one to this day.

With little to add to the work of the experts, we sadly packed it in and went back to Thailand. There was nothing we could accomplish, little we could do to help.

But, of course, the story stayed alive, as such mysteries will. The general shared what information and guidance we could develop with the Thompson company and his friends, with the family. I was the keeper of the file, maintainer of the records, collecting pieces and bits as they arose. Even as we returned to our official duties, the Thompson case hovered in the background. A good friend had been lost; the general was greatly saddened and wished to remain engaged.

Soon, in its exasperation at lack of any progress, the family back in the United States almost desperately sent out a celebrity psychic, Peter Hurkos, to apply his bamboozling magic to the case. We rolled up the eyebrows at the prospect, but of course promised support. What else could we do? The general asked me to work with Hurkos, help him as possible, keep an eye on him. Even as my leave or vacation time dwindled, I traveled once more to Malaysia with Hurkos where he was to work his voodoo and supposedly come up with a solution beyond the mere mortal powers of so many trackers, police, soldiers and others rather more familiar with conditions in faraway places with strange sounding names than was this amiable but nearly silly swami from Los Angeles.

An odd chap, Peter Hurkos. Immensely likeable in a thick-stew sort of way, he claimed to have been granted psychic powers after falling from a ladder and clanging his head on a cement floor. I have no doubt that his head had been influenced by landing on concrete after a fall, but I'm not sure I can entirely vouch for the psychic gifts. But there were others who swore by him. He'd worked various high profile crimes in America, including the then-famous Boston Strangler serial killings which I'd actually help cover as a cub reporter for the Boston Globe before coming into the Army. He came up with the wrong guy, as it happens, but he had lots of headlines out of it. The Thompson family hoped against hope that he would see something denied to the limited gifts of the hundreds of others already, but fruitlessly, involved.

Years within different cultures persuade me that there are many more things going on than we truly understand but I'm not sure that Peter Hurkos was the skeleton key to those things not understood – or whether he wasn't actually one of them himself. But he did have some sort of a gift – or, others might say, some sort of trick – that I never figured how he pulled it off. In his repertoire he had an interesting technique, which he worked on me for fun, and, later, on others, including a wealthy Bangkok widow and a Malaysian reporter who recognized me and who seemed likely to make a big deal of our return to the Cameron Highlands and stir up a new mess in the process. Hurkos would ask for a personal item, preferably a photo that we might have in our wallet, passed to him so that he couldn't see what it was, and he would proceed to tell us, purportedly from its aura and vibrations, about the person in the snapshot. Now, you could imagine that there were some pretty quick guesses anyone could make. The picture is likely to be of a loved one, a family member. A young person would likely have a photograph of a girl friend or boy friend. A little older person, it could be a child. There'd be a fifty percent chance on guessing the gender. And so forth.

He would start just like that, seeming so vague as to be appearing to shoot in the dark. But then he would move in on details that he couldn't possibly know or anticipate. Mine was of my fiancée, and he told me of what volunteer work she did and the size of her family and her interests. Guessable maybe somehow. With the Malaysian reporter he "read" that it was a picture of his brother, who was in school in Singapore, that they both mourned a sister who had married badly and moved away, that his wife had had a medical difficulty treated. And more. Interesting, certainly. And enough to buy the reporter's awed silence until we left town.

Which was good because Peter announced loudly and clearly that he had divined from the Cameron Highlands ether that Jim Thompson had voluntarily left with some CIA operatives and that they'd skittered off to murky western Cambodia where Thompson was secretly at work on a diplomatic solution to the Indochina war, headquartered in a temple out in the wilds where the Communists who would become the bloody Khmer Rouge rampaged. And nothing would do, he said, but that he and I must go there immediately.

Well, maybe not. This cooler head prevailed, imagining itself impaled on a Cambodian stake, a U.S. Army officer just dropping into that very, very dicey place. Instead we headed back to Bangkok, for "consultations" whereby Hurkos was finally discouraged from rambling around Sihanouk's messy kingdom and, much worse, Pol Pot's fatal neighborhood. So it was that Hurkos met an enormously rich and enormously beautiful American businesswoman who was reeling from the loss of her husband. He did paintings for her, god-awful things, I thought, dark and clotted. She loved it. He painted one for me, too. I still have it, in the back of a closet where it scares away ghosts and crawling creatures.

In Bangkok, waiting for things to sort themselves out – or maybe the family's money to dry up – Peter and I visited some of the more seedy nightclubs he cheerily favored and where he played his tricks on the bar girls, but never went beyond that with them. He was pretty well-behaved and genuinely pleasant for all his very rough-hewn corners and nearly total lack of social graces.

There, also, he somehow wrangled an audience with a noted Thai monk, widely known for his vast spiritual powers and ability to see what few others could see. I braced for the worst as we headed off to the temple to meet Phra Luang Phor Keo, whose august dignity and venerated reserve were a legend among the faithful. I hoped to be there to try to soften the impact of this heavy-handed, splintery-edged interloper, but I had misimagined the thing entirely: they got along wonderfully, two men as different as if being at farther ends of the species, sitting cross-legged on the floor of a rural temple, incense woozying me as chants and prayers could be heard in the background and the breeze tinkled the small brass bells in the rafters; they talked like old buddies about the state of the spirit and their varied lives and how complex is the role of barely significant man in a celestial system so rich with unknowable forces. They laughed and joked like old pals, or Army buddies. In all this, where somehow it was your pal, Denis, who was very much the odd man out, the thought wouldn't go away: "Toto, I have a feeling we're not in Dorchester anymore." The venerable monk had barely heard of Jim Thompson but had known vaguely that he had disappeared, probably carted away by local ruffians, and had no inkling where he might be.

Peter Hurkos went back to America and worked his Cambodia theories on the grieving relatives and others, but was little heard of again by us or those continuing the interest in the mystery.

There was never any news of what happened to Jim Thompson, as much as the case continued to fascinate over the years. Books are still being written about his disappearance, all these years later. My own unexciting theory was that he was kidnapped and that the bandits either killed him somewhere distant from the Moonlight Bungalow when things got so very hot or that he died in their hands and they just buried him, writing the case off as a bad investment. The kidnappings and ransoming in Malaysia were almost always done deep in the shadows, and the explosion of interest and grating attention might well have discouraged the bandits into cutting their losses and slinking away into their darkness. There's much to argue against that solution – notably that the rewards were so high it is likely that someone among the kidnappers would have come forward to squeal on the others, collecting the money and vanishing themselves. But nothing else much works to my thinking from the evidence.

I would so like to think that I'm simply wrong and that Thompson is, in fact, living with the female tribespeople, a nicer Lord Jim in his new world. I am totally sure his would be very entertaining native dinners around the campfire.

'Business' As Usual

BACK IN KORAT, life might have seemed somewhat tame compared to all the hijinks, and lowjinks, surrounding poor Jim Thompson. As it was, and as it always is, life is never tame, never dull, never boring. Looking for Jim and all the eccentric following-up took only a matter of a few weeks spread out over time, but the tendrils of the experience, like banyan tree roots, would silently weave forward to create for me a whole new reality lasting long after. Until this very instant, you could think.

The Army work was not something that was slowing down at all. The war continued to grow even when you could hardly imagine that it could get any bigger. The American military presence in Southeast Asia was expanding, with more and more war gear to be moved around to serve more and more missions. There were Thai troops to be trained, meetings with other U.S forces, with the Thai, with the Vietnamese, with the Air Force, with intelligence types whose associations were impenetrable, with SEATO. (Now, *there* was a racket, duty with the Bangkok-based Southeast Asia Treaty Organization which proudly accomplished pretty much nothing whatever but allowed its officers and staff to enjoy the good life with American holidays and Thai holidays and British holidays and Philippine holidays and Australian days off and so much more.)

We worked closely with the Thai army up-country, a professional-enough force that happily had little really to do, all in all. The country's leaders were all generals and field marshals with hundreds of ribbons on their chests but the Thai army had been little used over time. This is a good thing, particularly for the soldiers, but it discounted some the prospect that just because the military was large that it might also be a significant element of force. The soldiers trained well, although it was interesting at the least to work with grown men who would giggle, as was the cheery local custom from such happy people. For all its size, wealth and muscle, the Thai army might have been less of an actual power in the country than the Thai police, which were very much militarized and very tough – on their own people.

Although it had almost never fought anyone, the huge Thai Army was there and it brought in the gear and American aid that was pretty much just stock-piled lest it go to waste by being actually used; and, we knew, lots of the money was safely salted away in distant secret bank accounts by the generals for fear that the Thai humidity might well wrinkle the notes should they actually go to use otherwise for the expected reasons they were given.

The Thai officers and troops we had to deal with, though, did their job very well. Security from a much-exaggerated unfriendly element in the rural areas kept everyone safe and pilferage was minimal – in such sharp contrast to the situation in Vietnam where anything not nailed down, and a lot that was bolted down, disappeared in the dark of the night. Or in broad daylight. The Thais were so much better than that – corner cutters, to be sure, but pretty tame at it by the usual standards of the tinpot military governments the United States often dealt with. We generally felt that the nickel and dime stuff some were getting on the sly for their troubles was pretty small change against what they were risking. The Thai military culture was pretty well defined, one where rank had its privilege and privilege had most of the rank. But, as they say, it could have been worse. They had style, at least.

(Once, one of the Thai officers assigned to the general's headquarters to assist – and to keep an ear on us – pulled me aside and asked if I would do him a small favor, hardly anything at all. Seems he had a young cousin who was looking for a typist job; she was pretty good at English and excellent at office duties, he assured me. Just out of school was this little girl. But she was so shy and modest, such a sweet unassuming country girl, she didn't know how to apply properly for the work. Maybe I could talk her up to the hiring guys, he asked of the general's aide. There was a fair need for administrative help so it wasn't a crazy idea. Later he brought her around and she looked all of 12 years old, scrubbed up in her school uniform, hair back, make-up free, demure and, yes, shy. She got the job and did it well, I was told.

(Later, the officer invited me to his place for a drink after work, a pleasant invitation. So I showed up at his nice home on the edges of town and was served my glass of beer by the same young "cousin" now wearing a diaphanous tea bag of a dress and little else within, made up and coiffed like a movie star with an up-from-under-the-eyebrows glance that would freeze a bird in flight. A male bird, anyway. Very close with their kith and cousins, these Thais. Ah, well, she could type.)

In time, curiously even as when the war seemed ever increasingly to be going badly, the Thais set aside the fig leaf of the invisible American military presence. With a frank boldness and what could even appear a recklessness compared with the arch diplomatic minuetto they had preferred to dance so successfully for many centuries, the leadership in Bangkok came in with both feet against the Vietnamese Communists who so many knew would be around long after the Americans went home. Thailand sent a military unit, which we had been training and outfitting, to Vietnam. Several countries had units in Vietnam, often more for diplomatic impact than any significant military contribution; it allowed us to talk of the international flavor of our war there. Although none did less than was expected of them, expectations being wistful things, few did even more. Except, maybe, the South Koreans. At the U.S. military briefings I attended sitting in the back, on a drive-in-movie-sized map of the country the enemy forces were represented pretty much everywhere with little dots – except for one significant blank locale where the South Koreans were; the Viet Cong wanted nothing to do with the South Koreans, who would eat them, I think.

Though some said the quite competent and quite formidable Thais mostly did little more dangerous than risking straining their backs hauling stuff out of the U.S. PX system and making a mint selling their "Black Panther" patches to African-American GIs, the presence of troops in the war and the U.S. bases at home committed the Thai government to opposition with a powerful Vietnamese and Communist system already distinctly antithetical to that governing the Buddhist kingdom of Thailand root and branch, and one not very far away at all. There was a lot in it for the Thai military, of course, but there are easier ways to get tons of American money, supplies and armaments, without making even more of an enemy of the always-fighting Vietnamese.

But they were there in the fight and their government saw that as being in Thai interests. It also pointedly interwove those Thai interests to the conduct and success of the war, shackling the essential flexibility once seemingly inextricably gene-deep woven into Bangkok's traditional acceptance of the wisdom that in diplomacy the successful matador is seldom the one who stands directly in the path of the charging bull.

Of course the process began long before the Black Panthers division. It was increasingly impossible to ignore the shadow and activities of Americans across Thailand, at the peak flying monstrous B52s on bombing runs out of U-Tapao, the noisy conventional fighter-bombers, reconnaissance craft and tankers from so many other bases, uncountable trucks chugging up from the huge new port we built on the Gulf of Siam, the training bases, the pale, crewcut customers filling up the bars, and so much more. At no one crisp point was the magician's cloak of invisibility drawn away so much as what was once ignored was acknowledged with an air that suggested, "What? Those old things? You didn't know that they are here?"

Interestingly, more formal attention was directed to our service folks' leaving than was ever applied to their arriving – and no one made much of a point of wondering how these soldiers who were going home in the second place had got there in the first place. But old scamming habits die hard, as the world knows: Over time there would be grand pronunciamentos that would tell the world, "The Royal Thai Government and the United States government, reflecting the important progress in the Vietnam war, announce that 3,500 U.S. troops are leaving Thailand, reducing the presence to 38,000.... " Then, some months later another proclamation would be issued, "The Royal Thai Government and the United States government, reflecting the important progress in the Vietnam war, announce that 5,200 U.S. troops are leaving Thailand, reducing the presence to 38,000.... " There would always be 38,000 at the end of it. It was the miracle of the loaves and the fishes, in uniform. They would always leave, presumably, "on time," while others apparently slipped in by the back door.

Few enough of us were doing the woefully dangerous work that befell those truly valiant combat soldiers fighting and dying in such huge numbers for the politicians' and diplomats' despicable amusement; but everyone was part of the war in vital ways. Because each bomb that was delivered, each gallon of fuel that was made available to the jets, each trooper trained, each inch of new road constructed made the fighting that much more possible. For every hour on sentry, for every actually significant bit of paperwork that helped make the thing go, for every even distant element of the military spider web held in place by a man on duty in Korea or a woman working so well in Germany or Djibouti, all contributed something – for better or worse, and no matter how else one chooses to consider it – to the making of the great war in Vietnam, Laos and Cambodia. At the end of it, I was shruggingly comfortable that I had earned it when they gave me, along with my little tin badges for firing guns and being reasonably well behaved, a Vietnam service medal and ribbon.

Two, actually.

THE GAME IN THOSE DAYS was to do a year's duty and then go home. With the size of the Army and the horrendous extent and toll of the casualties for those enduring and risking them, the system felt that a year was plenty. But some had to do more and a few did more on purpose. That latter crowd included me.

Somewhere along the way I got it into my muggy head that I was actually doing interesting work, that the events at whose edges I flitted were vastly significant and demanded understanding, that the service I observed and even modestly performed was somewhat more important than the play-acting at life that I had innocently accomplished until then. I wondered if I might even dabble at it a bit longer. More, much more, there was in the Asian air something so exhilarating and fascinating to me, so incredibly different from anything I had seen before as to buoy the spirit, to invigorate the imagination. What work was ahead, anyway, that was so important as to be not disrupted? I had a few months left to my Asia assignment and then would be reassigned for busywork at some U.S. base in some dismal place (most military bases are built in dismal places) for the four or five months or so that would be left of my military time. I imagined that I could find my old reporting job at the Boston Globe waiting, as was the custom, when I returned from military duty – even if it were a little later than originally expected. Was there really anything much more significant to consider as being in the way should I somehow find the route to staying longer?

Oh, wait.

The wedding.

Well, yes, there was the little matter of the wedding.

All the while I was sporting around Southeast Asia seeing what I might see, I was engaged to the majestically good and beauteous Patricia Jeanne Alerding, herself originally a native of the same shaggy part of Boston as had hatched me. I had met her between college and reporting for the Army, and fell zippy for her in an instant. We dated. I simply could not believe my good fortune that she would allow so limited a character into her sunshine presence; I still cannot figure it out. In time, mirabile dictu, she agreed to marry me. Imagine that; I barely could.

Our plan was to marry immediately upon my completing the Asia duty, and about time it would be. ("Ah, Patsi," her parish priest had confided, in a conspiratorial whisper, "I've done you a favor." "What is that, Father?" "I've kept your name off the banns." "But why would you do that?" "Well ... well, because you're *so old*." She had just turned twenty-three, crone company in that simpler time when people did not wait through six careers and until Social Security loomed before marrying.) After the wedding, off we would go to where ever the Army wanted to send me for the dwindling months of the commitment. From there, surely, it would be back to civilization in Boston. While

I was soldiering away, she was working even harder on the wedding plans.

Yes, there was that.

But ideas so rarely occur to me that when one does pop to mind I tend to cling to it for a while.

Who can account for the things you do when you're only young? There was a great war going on that was killing people by the thousands each week, that was fracturing the American family, pitting the society against itself in high, corrosive anger, a war that was scalded by those who hated it and which was ferociously supported often by those who careed nothing of it but who hated the haters more than they hated the essentially pointless dying. Yet I was thinking of maneuvering to stay a part of such as that for another long year. Of course I was. Don't you have to gamble every once in a while to keep away the cobwebs?

Working the possibilities from different angles, I found that the Army, with the general's support, would let me sign up for a second tour in its Southeast Asia merriment, and wouldn't object if I went home in-between, married, then brought my new wife to Bangkok – and left her there. Actually, I never thought then to consider on what grounds they would try to halt me from doing just that anyway but, instead, was simply grateful that they went along with the plan.

Much more important, I found that Patricia thought that that would be an interesting thing to do – to leave your home and entire family, everything and everyone you've ever known, fly off with a guy you've just married after not having seen for more than a year to settle down mostly alone in an alien and exotic land where you knew no one, understood but little of the culture, language and climate, and had no idea whatever of how life would unfold in that distant place precisely on the other side of this round old globe of ours. Not at all a "whither thou goest ..." sort, she saw the adventure and excitement of the thing and was ready to give it a try. Amazing. Simply amazing.

So, wasting no time, I worked it all out. I went to the Army and re-upped, not all that difficult an accomplishment since there wasn't exactly a lot of hot competition for the opportunity to extend one's commitment in a war zone. As with Groucho's country club, maybe I could have been a little more skeptical about an outfit that welcomed in people addled enough to sign up for more of what so much of the rest of society was working so very hard to avoid; but my standards were diminished by the cheery prospects of learning and experiencing more of this wondrously bedeviling side of the planet. At a human level I was proud of the dedication, the strength, the sense of purpose and duty and the courage that so many, many people in the same uniform I was allowed to wear were showing, a world that had such different agendas at play than just those motivating the folks actually putting others in the such harm's way. These were no monsters, as so depicted in some harsh, ignorant quarters, nor were they all gods on the earth, as depicted by others equally remote from the reality; they were, mostly, good people doing a bum job that someone else sent them to do. So I asked to be allowed to stick around. Likely the Army itself was a bit distracted and had set aside uncommon sense entirely since they quickly gave the approval for me to be there and at it even longer.

Accordingly, before any minds might change, I organized up the travel, looked for a Bangkok apartment for Pat to stay in and the deal was done.

So it was that the following November I rocketed back to Boston, arrived on Dukes of Hazzard wheels just a few days before the ceremony, and we became Lt. and Mrs. Denis Horgan, Patricia Horgan and Denis Horgan. Everything was fittingly whirlwinded. And beautiful.

The very next morning, my birthday as it luckily happened, we left the United States and, like Vanderbilts, honeymooned in London, Paris and Rome. Quite unlike the Vanderbilts, though, we didn't have two dimes to do it with, but since the plane stopped in those grand cities on the way East, as was allowed back in those easier times, we hopped off for free and spent a few days in each grand town. Not a bad way to travel, although to my dazzled thinking, a honeymoon in Baluchistan, Newark or even Georgia would have been as wonderful in such company. And then, in a planet-engirdling hopscotch, it was on to Bangkok, where it was a.m. when the rest at home were in p.m., where the winter was embraceably steamy, the temples golden, the air alive with the flavors of the Orient and where nothing whatever was to be known about what tomorrow might bring – except that we would discover it alone and together, both.

We arrived, on time, to begin what should have been an odd but interesting year of this and that before furling the map and heading home once more. That was the plan, and it was a good one. I am so very good at making plans. Reality, though, is quite a bit better at unsettling them.

It would be perfectly clear to anyone why I had wanted to be in the same country, even the same time zone would have been better than before, with my lovely new wife, but we'll have to wait until she gets around to telling a tale of her own as to why she would think it a good idea to sail off to the other edge of the orb entirely, to be so distant from the family she loved, the friends she had accumulated by the hundreds and a way of life that had little like it in Krung Thep Mahanakhon Amon Rattanakosin Mahinthara Ayuthaya Mahadilok Phop Noppharat ... etc. etc. ... Bangkok. Imagine the leap of faith involved in such a thing. I had the Army all around me, colleagues and pals in some number, familiar facilities and language, an odd milieu, yes, but one in which I was inescapably a part. Pat chose the more grand gamble of living in a strange city and new culture as distant from anything she'd ever experienced than if she had landed on the Planet Pluto instead. Give her an attagirl and a thank you; I certainly did. And do.

CARTOGRAPHERS, PYTHAGOREANS and artillery targeteers likely could chart the distances from isolated points in the Thai northlands to the raspy but petal-strewn breezes of Bangkok in precise inches and centimeters, miles and meters. Good for them. But none has machines or formulas so sophisticated to measure the impossible new expanse in human terms that stretched out to divide the Thai capital from its dusty hinterlands or, more to the point, to separate me beyond the Issan horizon from Patricia in the big, big city below.

Suddenly so close, she now seemed farther away than even when we were never in the same a.m./p.m. moment with one another. Whatever we had thought or planned about living while being so close on the map rang out all hollow when she was just far enough beyond the grasp while seeming so near. So many others had it so much worse that it is merely insensitive to complain but, still, I could have better measured the leagues and hours to Bangkok in emptinesses, aches and sighs.

Pat had a job in an office, an apartment bubbling with international life, new young friends and the amazing challenges of discovering an entire opening culture. I had the continuing responsibilities of my own work, carrying out duties that were but pointillist bits of a huge picture barely comprehensible, doing what was necessary to move things along. I could work my way to Bangkok on the odd weekend, weekends in the military having little of the shape found elsewhere, and there was business to sometimes do there, too. It was fascinating for each of us, even as the distance was hardly needed to add much at all in the heart-growing-fonder department. We already had too much distance and we counted the days to its all ending according to the plan.

Trust the journalists, of course, to turn things upside down.

Thailand was a fairly busy place for newspaper guys and magazine folk and some TV sorts in those days. Many war correspondents, or sometimes their families, were based in Bangkok. And Thailand, for scribblers as well as soldiers, was a frequent R&R center for those seeking relief from Vietnam duty. They were a fascinating crowd, some cowboys along for the wild ride, others elbow-patched types airily looking for a Thucydidean imperative in it all; but mostly they were responsible, daring and hard-working – and not much likely to be distracted forever from the truth by the pawed-up gorilla dust of military officers looking to obscure things. Thailand was very much a sideshow to them, but some understood the complex Thai role in the war and came looking around. Many of those fell to me to squire about as the general, who was both media-savvy and well connected to that world, too, knew that reporters were best guided around rather than left stumbling around. I guess he figured I spoke the language – that of the journalists, if not so much that of the military or the Thais.

At one point a distinguished columnist and old pal to General Black, the cheery blueblood Rowland Evans, then famously but oddly the writing partner to the notoriously dark and malevolent Robert Novak, arrived on the scene gathering up information on the Vietnam War and its various extensions. We gave him the usual song and tap dance because he had holy water all over him, being a conservative supporter of the Vietnam festivities such as he was. And for being a friend to the general. So it was, the general tied up in a meeting, I was told to take him to a further up-country site where some sort of diverting mischief or the other took place. It would be an interesting field day to some activity not only of passing interest in the grander scheme but vital in its own way. And we could do it in a few hours by chopper.

Helicopters are such a neat way to travel. They fly low enough and slow enough to give a great view of the landscape; I was on a Huey helicopter probably five days a week and loved the special perspective as they thumped along, piloted by warrant officers – an odd breed ranking between commissioned officer and enlisted man who paid no particular attention to either. Because the helicopter made quite a racket, I could always daydream away as we flew over the world so close below, looking out the window and knowing that it was simply too noisy to have to listen to instructions or chitchat from all my superiors strapped into the din with me.

But this time as we were fluttering across the beautiful Thai ruralscape, long green and light brown checkerboards of rice paddies with sudden clusters of trees like eyebrows here and there, with the sun sparkling off the golden nagas or serpents on the red-roofed temples popping out of the flatlands, the machine began to shake and wobble. This is seldom a good thing. Helicopters, wingless, tend not to glide to the ground when they don't work anymore. Rather, they sort of careen in and, with the long whirling rotors, anything but a truly flat arrival could lead to a quite messy flipover. It is not considered career enhancing to be in a helicopter tumbling to the ground. The pilot told us there was a problem and we were going to have put down someplace quickly. Good idea. After a bit of lurching, he said there was an airstrip just ahead and we should be able to make that. I didn't know of any airstrip out there but it looked mighty welcome to me; any airstrip in a pinch, I always say. But even as we coasted into the place I knew we were in a different kind of trouble. Well, that *I* was in trouble.

As I watched out the window, we rocked and rolled onto an airstrip along which were parked the strangest airplanes I had ever seen, all unmarked. There were small planes with big bubbles on them like the Pope's limo; aircraft with stumpy wings with great lengths of wire and tall aerials sticking out all over the place; machines with enormous tires, others with vertical V-shaped wings. There might have been a flying saucer there and I missed it, but I wouldn't have been surprised. This, I thought, is not yonder Don Muang airport where the punctual tourists arrive to the sound of light flutey music and happy welcomes and flowers around the neck. We hadn't even clanked onto to the ground before our chopper was surrounded by three jeeps full of very stern looking men, who demanded that we stay inside our machine, cooking in the Southeast Asian sun. You bet, boys.

Finally a man with a colonel's eagle loosely pinned onto a shirt that looked like something he didn't wear very often but with no other service designation or insignia whatever came out and brought us to a large windowless shed where he exchanged the charm with Evans about the loveliness of the weather and various other empty things until another helicopter arrived to get us the hell out of there, clearly a misty spook center of some sort.

"Now, Mr. Evans," I allowed later with a cornpone shuffle. "I'm kind of thinking that maybe this place was sort of secret and maybe not something that you should have seen, and maybe you could ..."

"Oh, don't worry," he said in an understanding, if wispy and lofty way, eyebrows akimbo. "I'm not *that* kind of journalist." Whatever that meant.

Of course everyone was yapping at me afterwards for bringing him there, as if I had written him an AAA TripTik, for allowing a *god-damned* newspaper man into a *blickety-blank* highly classified base and what the *brazzlefritzin'* hell would they say to headquarters about that, you dope. I allowed as they might want to tell headquarters that the helicopter pilot did a really good job in getting us down from the skies safely, considering that thin-skinned choppers have a tendency to fall rather like an anvil when the power's off, thus likely saving the limbs and life of the famous journalist and the two-for-a-dollar young lieutenant in the process, since precious little good was likely to come from having us all killed. Begrudgingly, they conceded the merits of saving the pilot and at least half of that passenger list. The warrant officer just buffed his nails as the sparks flew my way. Helicopter pilots were not going to let much distract them from having a pleasant tour in Thailand, since their vital occupation insisted that they'd be back in Vietnam very, very soon where the problem is less often where you land but what bad news probably brought you to come down at all. Cranky bosses? Big deal, says they.

I never found out what that base was all about. There were odd games going on all over the place, and it was hardly likely that even side-kicking for an important general would allow me to figure out much of it. The "McNamara Wall" of electronic eavesdropping pellets scattered across Laos to catalog traffic on the Ho Chi Minh Trail required attention and monitoring by its keepers. The archly secret Air America work of the CIA in Laos and Thailand was so archly secret that they were openly, simply called "CIA Air" and you could pick the pilots out of a line-up – and often had to, them not exactly being West Pointers, socialites, clerics and all; they even made a movie about it when the war was largely still going on. Some secret. Strangers would arrive looking like Australian kangaroo herders, or whatever they do in Australia, and have long meetings to which I was pointedly not invited. Small planes would arrive in the dark of the night, which was already odd, and we would pick up some stone-silent fellow who would vanish in the morning before I could even get in a baseball bet, and he was as gone as if he had never been there. And I never knew what it was that we were doing with the Khmer Seri in Cambodia, getting shepherd-crooked out of any meeting where that came up, even as I might otherwise be doodling the crosswords when other items of sky-high security or diplomatic intrigue were being discussed.

Reporters and other newspeople would get the vaudeville act briefings if they wanted, but, on the face of it, we were pretty thin news gruel compared to the very hot war banquet available for the picking in the neighborhood. People could travel around the country pretty much on their own if they thought of it, likely with a Thai police shadow, and there were always some out looking for the phantom Thai communists alleged to be slithering around imperiling the future of the kingdom. I never heard that any were found by the journalists out hunting for them. Or by the military. We were assured that there were some out there hatching dark plots against us and our Thai hosts, but I never saw any evidence of it in any meaningful way, which hardly stopped the Thai military from shaking the U.S. equipment tree for all sorts of extra gear, arms, supplies and cash to battle the dark menace. The word to us was to treat the journalists warily but well. As with Rowlie Evans' airfield adventure, it was better to play it cool than to get all fritzy and raise too many new questions.

Mostly, reporters were considered only a pain in the neck by the brass. But there were exceptions, of course. Another time, on a visit to a really remote unit of the command, I was shaken from a deep sleep and ordered in the sharpest wake-up tones to get my Frankenstein's creature self to the nearest telephone – at a fairly distant air base as it happened – to await a vital and important call. The suggestion was that my balsa wood head would roll if I failed to be there. My, my. What was this all about? But off I went, imagining that the President was surely calling seeking my advice on some complex matter, or maybe Miss Apasra was on the line wondering how I was liking her Thailand and mightn't I like to drop by for lemonade some afternoon

... things like that.

When the phone call was finally patched through, and you could hear it coming link by link from Washington to the faraway reaches of northeast Siam, from the Pentagon switchboard to CINCPAC in Hawaii to MACTHAI in Bangkok and USARSUPTHAI in Korat and hopping and scotching to me in the boonies, a brisk woman identified herself as a fact checker for my now-favorite magazine, the National Geographic, and insisted in first sergeant tones, grilling me like a district attorney, to know whether I had, in fact, said that the sun came up in the east or that soldiers often wore boots or some such simple thing. Well, I guessed that, yes, I had said that. Thank you, and she hung up.

Some months before, the pleasant and indefatigable Robert Jordan of the Geographic had passed through the hemisphere working on a huge cover story about the state of the United States Army. Of course, the United States Army would have hauled him around in a sedan chair hefted by young officers like me if he had wanted, so interested was it in making sure he remained a happy fellow and that he would write nice things about the service. He was a happy fellow in his own right, extremely nice, and his run through Thailand with me at his elbow barely warranted a nameless clause in his account; but the researchers and fact-checkers were far more thorough than even the subject of his writing in doing their job. Very impressive. With the time difference, the day was done for poor old me, so I figured the best thing was to just to go back to bed. And I didn't even get any insider dope that I could parlay into a bet or a bit of gossip worth a drink at the officers' club bar.

Much more consequential, to me, at least, more than cloud-scraping columnists or warm-windy stories in the Grand Geographic, was the arrival into my life of one Alessandro Casella.

HERE IT WAS THAT THE CONTINUING LEGACY of Jim Thompson grabbed me with both hands by the collar, picked me up into the air and placed me ultimately on a different road entirely than any I might have envisioned, even under the pickling influence of Thailand's mind-bending beer.

Even while there were no actual developments in the Thompson disappearance – and have been none over the decades since – Jim's friends and colleagues in Bangkok and beyond sustained their interest in the strange case. Why wouldn't they? An important star in their galaxy had winked out. He was their friend. He was one of them. They cared. If nothing else, there was the grand mystery of it all. Business people, government officials and, not the least, General Black occasionally met, socially and professionally, to update one another on the latest rumors – or frustrations. The general thus found himself floating through a company rather different from the boys in military hues who so dominated his time and energies otherwise. My invitations to these thin-air social sessions were somehow lost in the mail, although the general would keep me informed, and I would update the file if necessary. What proved critical to me, if not necessarily to poor Jim Thompson, was that Ed Black was moving with a different crew in different circles than usually was the case.

One such new acquaintance was Giorgio Berlingieri, whose Ital-Thai Corporation did major road-building work with the U.S. government, built tall buildings in Bangkok, had salvaged vessels sunk in the harbors and rivers, owned the elegant Oriental Hotel on the Chao Phrya riverside and whose fingers were deep in a variety of other endeavors. A majestically amiable character, full of acumen, intelligence, sophistication and great spirit, Giorgio's Ital-Thai also just happened to own the Bangkok World newspaper.

If he even needed the emphasis, Berlingieri certainly saw the significance of being friendly with an American general whose forces were engaged in exactly the construction efforts that his construction company specialized in – even as it was his fashion to be friendly and elegantly expansive in any case.

One day the general said to me, in passing, "My friend Giorgio tells me he's hired a new editor at the Bangkok World, a Swiss guy. Maybe if you run into him you could see what he's like. Just check him out so I can have something to say if Giorgio mentions him again. Don't get us involved."

The "don't get us involved" part was the general's way of saying, "don't do anything stupid" since I was an Army officer after all, actually a captain by this point.

Now, the difference between a run-of-the-mill aide and a world-twirling wizard such as I was is that the former follows the letter of the rules, sees clearly but dimly the limits and stays smartly within them while the dazzler and brain-heavy other hears the spaces between the notes, understands the eloquences there are in the silence, reads what isn't yet written and conjures from the thinness of the air what hasn't quite been said. Anticipation rather than reaction. Inspiration rather than plodding discipline.

"Maybe if you run into him you could see what he's like. Just check him out so I can have something to say if Giorgio mentions him again." Okie doke, boss. Didn't I exactly know what the general truly was instructing me? I hardly needed a billboard to read the command on the wall. If you took that *maybe if you run into him* and held it up to the sun and scrunched your left eye shut just so, it could be seen as a suggestion to go down to Bangkok when the chance came up – or was manipulated to come up – and help out the general in his dealings with a major contractor and consequential new friend and if, well, it also allowed me a chance to say "how-do-you-do" to my otherwise distant wife, why that would be simply an amazing but welcome coincidence.

So I just happened to find my way to Bangkok and the newspaper's offices on some quasi business or another and stuck out the paw to Sacha Casella who was just settling in as the new editor of the World.

Sacha was, indeed, "a Swiss guy" – an Italian, actually, who had emigrated to Switzerland – about five years older than I was and who had landed at the Bangkok World after some years of reporting and writing about Asian events from Vietnam and Europe. He was scholarly and nuanced, but no ivory tower denizen at all. He understood what he knew because he had gotten out there and discovered it for himself. His earlier acquaintance in Saigon with a French businessman, Charles Regnault, himself by now the key deputy to Giorgio Berlingieri, opened the door for him to English-language journalism in Thailand. Casella was smart and well-educated (not always the same thing), deeply steeped in Asian affairs, archly cynical, wry and keenly aware of the unending and shape-shifting flows of Southeast Asian currents – largely, to his credit, because his integrity and cheery disdain for the rules ran him afoul of so many of them.

We hit it off immediately.

An amazing storyteller, Sacha's shared grand tales and observations of the war, of personalities and policies tripping over themselves in mad competition to do the thing that would seemingly least likely work. One of those people who annoyingly could speak every language he tried, his briskly European perspective gave him a vital prism on the region's swirling history and events, little tinted by the intense local interests of the Southeast Asian or American influences and allegiances. Sacha had the sense of the very long haul that was so little respected in the quick-answer world of the blood-drenched moment. He saw the long range import of China's people-hammering path from misery to poverty and the direction it could carry them, to the consequence of the rest of the world: sooner rather than later, certainly sooner rather than never, as the bad-wishful-thinkers would prefer it. He was keen to the diplomatic vanities of so many of the actors in the great drama of the day, even as his own politics might make him an odd peg for the curious holes of Thai military and daily official reality, forces not much comfortable with criticism or second-guessing.

Whether he was particularly equipped to thread the maddening complexities of producing a daily newspaper from the raw materials available in Bangkok, Thailand, might be another tough question entirely, but he was certainly enthusiastic and ready to try his very best, this when you could anticipate that his views were likely to land him in Thai hot water sooner or later. As I say, we hit it off immediately.

Back in the northeast later, I told the general that I had met with Casella and was impressed with Berlingieri's choice, but marveled at the challenges he faced in the day-to-day complications sure to arise in the mechanics of Pied Pipering a newspaper through the Thai labyrinth. Distractedly while shaving, pretending that his mind was on other deeply military matters, Black said something like, "That's nice. I hope it works out."

Aha.

Knowing the general so well, I was quite persuaded that what he meant for me to hear and absolutely would have said had he focused more intently through the dilapidation that I was sure afflicted everyone of his vast age so soon after the half-century mark, was: "That's nice. Help him out if you can, but on your own, even if that means you will have to take time from the warm pleasures of the often arid and grainy and clotted north to go down to the distracting, temple-bespeckled, exotic, bewitching Bangkok where your young bride just happens to be." A good soldier, I saluted smartly at his unspoken command – and likely as yet unformed thought – and slid down to Krung

Thep by bus or truck on what days off I had and as a sideline to actual business while there and, in passing, kept up the contact with Sacha Casella at the World. I even toured him a little around the northeast, with an eye to assuring him that we were not boiling Thai children in big cannibal pots. On one visit he even got to watch me nearly get killed in a major-league jeep accident.

Over time I am happy to know we became friends, a friendship that has stayed with us even as our lives, careers, families and fortunes have wended every which way since. We talked about newspapering, about Thai politics, about Asian twists and swirls, about life and friendships and events near and far. We shared our experiences, swapped advice. It was beyond my place, or beyond any inclination, to suggest that he might temper a bit his bold views on the sensitive local policies and military leaders who were quite capable of gnawing off his leg; as it was, I might just as well have suggested that he don a hula skirt and dance the fandango. But I think there might have been a few things I offered that were dimly helpful in considering how a multinational newsroom might get through the week without too much bloodshed or mutiny.

Particularly, we discussed newspapering, the Thai sensibilities in the workplace, manners of motivation and inspiration of writers and editors, each of whom thinks he or she has the key to all wisdom and would be rich himself if he could only be rid of all the lunatics who bog him down in his poetry – and if he could buy the proper lottery ticket. We talked about how newspaper stories might be made to dance, how important photographs are to telling the tale. We discussed how best to use the pages, what sort of audience there was to read an English-language newspaper in Thailand and what it might be looking to find in such a thing. We made small talk about great matters and great discourse on tiny things, the essence of journalism. The importances of flow and rhythms in reporting and storytelling, the acceptability on the page of the mundane if it enlivens, illuminates, the miniscule in a season of gigantic developments, the value of humor and the funnies. Such as that we discussed over wine on the riverside terrace of the Oriental Hotel or in the poolside gardens of the Erawan Hotel, or over dinner with Pat. It was great fun, and maybe helpful.

In any event, as the months passed, Alessandro Casella, chief cheese of the Bangkok World newsroom, finally wondered whether I mightn't be interested in staying on in Thailand when my military time soon ran out and becoming , what?, pick a title, managing editor?, managing editor of the paper.

522 Phrasumaine Road

Up in Korat when General Black would read through the Bangkok papers he would often cast his practiced eye – a peeper buffed to sharpness from OSS work decades before and by a rich career watching the sparrow-falling signs of the military's outsized, frothy bureaucracy at "work" – over the articles looking for hidden nuggets of sly information. He would scan the shipping reports and idly catalog who was active at the city's busy port, which nation seemed to have more vessels in the local water than the rice and light manufacturing trade might support. He would study the social notes to track the dancing diplomats. And he would analyze the local political news for signs of what straws might be floating along in the wind, who was up, who might be on the way down. Particularly, he was alert to a recurring column by Manoj Vudha in the Bangkok World which summarized items wrapped up from the vibrant, zippy Thai-language newspapers.

"He's sending a message," Black would say again and again of Manoj's curious work. "Listen to this: 'Thai Rath opines favorably, inter alia, that what is outbound on major arteries is a great concern while Prajamitra maintains, ab initio, that the voices of the east bode a hot season ahead – and we are wise to keep an eye, ipso facto, on how the breeze ruffles the crops. Meantime, M.R. Kukrit Pramoj at Siam Rath editorializes about delays in peaches, sine die, which distress him enormously.'

"What in blazes does that mean?," the general would wonder. "And here he is again, 'Many journals did not write about the deer that was not seen at Lumpini Park.' I tell you there's a code in this!"

Well, we read them and studied them and held them up to the light at different angles, and couldn't figure out what important message Manoj was sending, or to whom. Some of the command's finest minds were on the case, not always a pretty picture.

One day, though, visiting the Bangkok World's offices to call on Sacha Casella, whom do I run into delivering his latest report but Manoj Vudha himself. I was introduced to this very elegant, charming, grey-haired man, dressed in blue-blazer perfection as he always was, with his tie set in a very large double-Windsor knot, light maroon handkerchief in crisp pocket square, and who said to me in his soft, courtly way, "I am pleased, inter alia, to meet you. The papers were very quiet again this week, in res maligno, but the holes in the road deepen and the wind, heed me well, is heavy with the dew from the west. I have not seen a deer in Lumpini Park in many years, have you? And it continues to surprise me that no one writes about that ..."

There was no code, it was just the way Manoj spoke. I never disabused the general of his hope that he had discovered some encrypto-communications lode buried in the column. It was far more fun to imagine him – and the finest minds in the APO code – deep on the case, looking for meaning where only addled English was the case. It is always best to divert the military's finest minds to cul-de-sacs, where they can do less damage.

You could get quite a headache trying to read things into the Bangkok World. Indeed, you could get quite a headache in those days just from reading the Bangkok World itself. The newspaper was not what you might consider attractive; or friendly looking. It did its best – and a mighty "best" that was, so many blasted things considered – but the type tended to wriggle like that found low on an eye-chart, wandering around like a drunken man trying to find his way home but whose suspenders have snagged on a doorknob; there were fewer straight lines than in a barrel of ping pong balls. It had a blocky look to it and sometimes a letter in a headline seemed to be rising up a bit from the others, or dipping below, as if trying to escape a conga line. There were typos in half the sentences, where an "m" would fall into the place where a "w" might be expected, where a "g" seemed a suitable substitute for a "j' should the "j" have gone off on vacation.

It was, you see, – or, more likely, as you have *never* seen – a newspaper put together entirely in handset type. Just like in Ben Franklin's day. Well, in Ben's day if Poor Richard had Thai typesetters who didn't really know a "C" from a "G" or that the humpy thing the writer had meant to be an "n" was not precisely the same thing as the upside-down "u" that their nimble fingers extracted from the large type trays, character by character. At the end of the day all that type, held together by string, would be washed and broken down and sorted back into those trays, one by one once more, into the tiny little boxes where a "1" would very well wander over to visit with the "l" and the "7" and the question mark would chit-chat together over such things as interest small bits of lead thrown together unceremoniously. Because it is type, it would be put into the pages upside down and backwards, so the miscues, or misQs, or wisos, were not easily caught, but that made no difference to the Thai compositors as they couldn't read English anyway.

The Bangkok World was only ten years or so old when I first joined it, but it had the eccentric quality of looking ten times more ancient than that. Linotypes and the beginnings of electronic typesetting might exist elsewhere in the printing universe, but they were not to be found at 522 Phrasumaine Road. Perversely, maybe, the quill & ink look of the newspaper was made brilliantly sharp and clear running, as it did, through the excellent Japanese presses brought to Thailand two decades before during the Second World War occupation to print propaganda. Each smudge and nomad consonant was printed in brisk relief, for all to see.

Because it was Asia in the 1960's, the worn-out look of the thing appeared less startling than you might expect and, in fact, had a certain retro charm to it. It gave the comfortable reader, plush in his or her easy English-speaking lifestyle with housemaids and drivers and the wealth of the rajahs compared to that of those locals around, a sense of quaint exoticism. It probably also gave them eyestrain. They had no idea of the daily typographical marvel that found its way into their hands, and shouldn't have had to: very few appreciate what a glorious thing is a newspaper, no matter where and how it is made. No one not on the payroll gives a thought to how all the words they read come to snuggle together, however clumsily. Bill Harting would soon come along and show us how to design a page that did not so mirror the look of those hauled together by Horace Greeley, and new machines would be finally brought in to set the type in new-fangled modernity – but a warm part of me never really wanted to acknowledge the improvement from the charmingly quirky, even goofy, look of what was so amazingly unique, so amazingly ours.

The Bangkok World was launched in 1957 by Darrell Berrigan, one of those merry freebooters – as was Jim Thompson and so many others – who rattled around the planet after the Second World War to try their hands at all manner of interesting things that were so much more compelling than all the plodding chores waiting patiently at home, that were so much more pleasant than what the earth had endured so recently in its grinding obsession in finding new ways to have wars, in

new places and with new toys of doom. Berrigan, like Alexander Mac-
Donald, who had set up the original Bangkok Post a decade earlier,
found it hard to go back to the safe and sound life that the wars and
depressions had so upended – but ultimately sustained. MacDonald
soon enough did go home; Berrigan did not.

MacDonald's Post had long since been taken over by England's
Thomson chain, which inflicted its silly and odd spellings and Chau-
cerian Britishisms on the defenseless readers. Berrigan, legendarily
with the financial help of a Thai police general and the presumed
moral support at least of the American embassy, which lamented the
lack of baseball scores, started the Bangkok World as a small opportunity to find a niche in the expatriate and better-educated Thai communities. It's what people could do in those days.

While we may never know what happened to poor Jim Thompson
in Malaysia, we know what happened to Darrell Berrigan in Bangkok.
He was murdered in 1965, shot dead in the dark of night in an incident
involving young homosexual streetwalkers. It was a sensational matter,
especially sensational to no one more than to poor Darrell Berrigan,
of course. The World and the Post covered it in respectful solemnity,
while the Thai press happily jazzed-up the grim and grisly details,
which barely needed jazzing, eager to make a very large thing indeed
of the tawdry doings and sad results for such a prominent farang, as
all westerners in the community were known, a linguistic application of "French" by the Thai to all Europeans and Americans since,
of course, you could barely tell one from another anyway. The paper
stumbled along for the next few years, coming into the hands of Ital-
Thai and, after a few others, the editorship of Sacha Casella in 1968.
Shortly later, I joined the paper, more than a little pop-eyed at the way
events had unfolded. In the most unbecoming manner allowable under
the laws of the military and those of the heart, I warmly hugged Briga-

dier General Edwin Fahey Black, saluted everyone else in sight in the Army as my duty ended, and, with the astonishing concurrence of my wife, already far more a Krung Thep resident-veteran than I was, became managing editor of the Bangkok World.

I HAD BEEN A MANAGING EDITOR BEFORE: For our slim college weekly newspaper, with its volunteer staff of a dozen or so students. I had studied journalism at both the undergraduate and graduate levels, but studying journalism and committing acts of journalism are as different as reading about first aid in the Cub Scout manual and being handed the scalpel in the operating theater. In classrooms they instructed me on the refinements of the Sullivan and Zenger defenses and obscure legalisms once at play in ye ancient day of the old New England colonies. I think they taught me something about how to write a story so as to deliver its point before the second jump, but I don't recall that they lost an hour on consideration of how to gather up the news and information that went into the story. As a kid reporter later at the Boston Globe, I was once part of a team rushed to an incredible fire at a large school as it totally burned in the night, aeried atop a hill with its every window fiery red and with flames leaping to the moon. I could have written a poem about that fire, so spectacular a sight it was, but my professors would have been astonished to learn that there was little demand for poetry about fires back in the newsroom. No one had taught me in school how to cover the fire itself, whom to ask what questions, where to find out information as reality sizzled all around me. I learned pretty quickly from the doing of it, that most efficient of teachers.

But it's not as if I had anticipated or expected very much from the universities in the way of direction, if I had been envisioning myself as a newspaper guy. In fact, I had never at all envisioned myself as a newspaper guy. In those days, no one in his right mind did. It would happen later that the journalism universe would come to acquire a brief generation's worth of high glamour and, in odd circles, respect. Young people would have their cottony noggins stuffed with visions of the noble calling, the great good to be done, the zip and swagger of strolling along with the mighty. Practitioners would be promoted from "newspaper guy" to "journalist" to part of the "media" for doing pretty much exactly the same job. The newsrooms became infested with highly educated young visionaries and extremely well educated reporters, lofty minded souls who actually paid for their own drinks sometimes.

But in my time, doing newspapering had still an air inviting icy disdain and contempt for the "Front Page" rascality of a nest of scoundrels slathered with a social opprobrium richly earned and casually welcomed in its 24-karat abundance. It was, purely and surely, The Good Old Days. I did not set out to become a newspaper guy any more than someone sets out to be an alcoholic or drug addict; it happens that many of us might end up that way but no one starts out with that as The Plan. There would come a time later, before the industry withered, when honest young people actually imagined being Woodward & Bernstein or even Lois Lane, of being elbow-rubbers with the worthy, respected citizens of some esteem. But not back then; not in my formative time.

As with almost everything into which my big feet would carry me, I stumbled into newspaper work. It was all pretty much an accident. Thank heavens.

I had no idea what to do with my life at the moment when I was supposed to make just those critical decisions that would shape the entire future, guide my career out into my dotage. When they demanded that I make the college call as to what road I was choosing to travel forevermore, I drew a blank. At age 18, I was only on the high end of being a sap adolescent rather than the low end of being a responsible adult. How was I to know what to do with the rest of my entire days? Yet they demanded an answer. As when the Army wanted me to choose a destination for my duties, I was without a single smart thought as to what I should study in college, if I could find one with low-enough standards to take me in. We had no guidance counselors in those distant days, and no one ever had anything to do with the school bosses anyway unless you were in deep trouble. The only counsel we were provided was to be told to shut up and make no trouble for the system. No one advised on the merits of macro-historical imperatives or architecture or pharmacy as a line of life. I suppose you were meant to stumble along until something fit. Stumbling along was something I was pretty good at.

I did have it squarely in my head that I must find a career that had no mathematics in it. I did not believe in math then and, after a lifetime of experience all around the planet, I do not believe in it now. Mathematics – arithmetic, even – is merely a cruel hoax conjured up by teachers to break the poetical spirit of the young: just when the head fills with happy, daydreamy aspirations towards vapid nothingness and warm thoughts of romance abudding, the cruel teachers throw a lump of geometry at one's poor skull. Mathematics has no other practical purpose, and I have visited seven of the eight corners of the globe and not once has anyone ever asked me to do a square root. Or to read a cosine. Plus, it is all very hard, being nonsensical to begin with.

So it was that I shopped around for a college run out of the back of a van, a university dedicated to standards so jellylike as to allow anyone in, one with programs where I would have to endure no mathematics whatever. I knew what not to do; what to do instead remained a mystery. I did know I liked to write, and appreciated that teachers, when not math-gnarled themselves, were easily diverted by someone's having some small sense of sentence structure and who might have actually read the book being talked about. But there is no great career in bamboozling teachers. What to do with writing? I liked the abstract quality of poetry as it didn't seem to take much work to string out a few lines that only sometimes rhymed. But what was the future in being a poet? Everyone talked so romantically about the life of "the starving poet" but I did not see the great advantage of a career where "starving" was part of the job description. Write novels? Yes, people did that. But what did I know enough about to haul along for hundreds of pages, even as so many others did so anyway? Nothing, that's what. Wait. How about advertising? They used writing in that. Not even a lot of it. Yes, that's the ticket. Write a few words – "Drink Coke" – and make a bundle. So I tricked my way into Northeastern University's school of business administration to become an advertising man, which was becoming all the rage. Good plan.

Except that I quickly found to my horror that the school of business administration is perfectly awash in mathematics: statistics, accounting, economics and the ghastly like. Why hadn't someone warned me? Everywhere I turned there were numbers, tables, facts and figures that I was supposed to master. I had made a terrible mistake and could see no way out.

But, of course, there is always a way out.

Taking an English course with the business administration chain gang, I caught the weary eye of the young teaching assistant assigned as part of some parole arrangement to try to press literature on prospective accountants and marketers. Those chalky knuckledraggers, in turn, liked his English the way I liked their math, and the instructor, a Mr. Connolly, apparently welcomed my island of interest in the sea of frozen, dead-eye faces before him. He was startled to discover that I had actually read the works he assigned. He seemed amazed that I could even be inspired to understand things that do not have rows of numbers in them, that I enjoyed, where no one around us did, these books and stories, these poems and ideas.

In time he asked me The Deep Question: "What are you doing here?" It was not some universal Buddhist soul assessment such as I would later encounter in more misty surroundings, temples and saloons, but, instead, "What on earth are you doing so unhappily studying business where you have no aptitude or prospect whatever?" I told him of my misdirection and, mulling it, he wondered whether I hadn't ever considered the college of liberal arts instead. I had not. I assumed that was some political outfit and hadn't much noticed it at all. So he marched me across the concrete campus to the college of the liberal artists where a friend of his grilled me like a bomb-defuser before, himself, asking, "Have you ever thought of writing for a newspaper?"

Writing for a newspaper?

No, I had not.

Of course I hadn't thought of that. Not for one second had I considered it, even as the house was knee-deep in newspapers. In those grand times, Boston had at least six daily newspapers going, and more if you counted the old Christian Science Monitor which was something of a daily magazine and which, astonishingly and unworthily, had no funnies. And we had almost all of these newspapers at home because my father would bring them back from work or from the subway. I read them all; I could keep track of all the hundreds of comic strips when I couldn't keep track of the name of who was the governor or mayor, being just as likely to miss by as much as two-thirds when called upon to name my brother and sisters; I knew the best writers to read in the sports sections and which papers had the best editorial cartoons. I could wear out a pencil doing all of the crossword puzzles, but I had never once thought that someone actually wrote those newspapers into existence. Truly. And no one bothered to so inform me because, you see, newspapering was so beneath social contempt and newspaper people, you should understand, were still very much considered society's dregs and outcasts, deservedly so in the wan view of the haughty scholarly world such as afflicted and wrung to powder the souls of the young in its skeletal hands.

Writing for a newspaper.

Imagine that.

I hadn't.

Through the school's cooperative work program, I was assigned a job as a copy boy at the Boston Globe. They don't have such things as copy boys anymore, but it was the lowest position imaginable in a hierarchy that, frankly, never stretched very high. But that was fine with me. I first walked into the vast Globe newsroom and was genuinely startled to see all kinds of mayhem, people shouting, the brisk smell of alcohol in the air, swearing and cursing from people with cigarettes dangling from their lips under sweat-stained fedoras, shouting matches exploding, fists being shaken. And that was just the religion writing crew. Everywhere there seemed to be mad chaos, electric confusion, elbows flying, rudeness, intemperance and bawdiness. I fell in love.

Dazzled, I went home and said to my ancient father, "Dad, I have decided not to pursue a life in business as you had hoped but, instead, I am going to become a newspaper guy."

The poor man fell over onto the floor in a faint. *Plop.* We propped him up in a chair and poured whiskey into his mouth – which had nothing to do with the faint but was, instead, just what we always did with him. Coming to, he said, with operatic sadness, "A newspaper man? My son, you will be associating with the swamp dwellers of society, the outcasts, the worst actors, the lowlives, criminals and degenerates. And by that I mean your fellow newsmen, not the poor people you write about." Yes. That was exactly my goal. I was in with both feet and my dispirited father sensed it.

I don't think, as hard as he tried, that he ever got over what he lamented as my dismal choice. Even as I advanced to thin air opportunities in the game, he always held onto hope that I would come to my senses and go straight. I was nearly a favored son; second best, at the least. Out of two. But he would introduce the family at events: "This is my oldest boy. He's just got out of prison and has a fair chance of staying straight for a week or so. And this is my daughter, she lives in a box under a bridge – but it's quite a nice box. And ... this is Denis. He works ..." he would then cover his mouth with a handkerchief and mumble ... "as a *m*mbrtz%nn*," which a bat or sonar operator might make out as, "a newspaper man." Often, with the deepest sighs, he would tell me I was "a disgrace to the family name." Me? The family name? This was a family alive with racketeers, arsonists, horse thieves, attorneys, pickpockets, yet somehow I was the one who was the disgrace.

But that was all right. I was having fun. I was a copy boy. Being a copy boy and being a managing editor were not precisely the same things and managing editors could be forgiven for envying my job. I would sit around until some ancient would yell "copy!" and then rush forward and grab a piece of paper and bring it to the composing room. Or I would run other errands and fetch coffee for people who would sometimes offer me a five-cent tip. I would paste bits of paper on other bits of paper, for some strange reason. I would distribute the mail, deliver messages, answer the phone. Between these weighty assignments, I would watch the newsroom drama play out before my dazzled eyes. Grown men barking at one another. Grown women baying at one another. Bells going off for no reason I could ever calculate. Dozens of typewriters clicking and phones ringing, volcanoes of noise and hurricanes of energy whirling all around. And they actually paid me to be there, instead of asking me to buy a ticket as I willingly might have done for far less exciting entertainment elsewhere. In time, working nights while going to school days, I wrangled an internship and then a cub reporter's spot on the staff. I covered fires. I wrote about car crashes. Shootings. Obits. Robberies. Murders. It was wonderful.

I did not write about politics. Or education trends. Or science. Or review books. In the Globe of those days there was a caste system more vivid than that of bedotted India. One half of the newsroom was made up of the Irish Gang – people named Monaghan, Callahan, Doyle, O'Brien, Nolan, Anglin, Horgan, Bucko Smith and Connie Noonan. Our assignment was life's coffee grounds, the scratching of people up against each other with bloody-nose results. The pain and trouble. The raw life. On the other side of the room, across a DMZ as distinct as that at the 38th Parallel, was the dainty Harvard Gang, people with last names for first names and Roman numerals in their by-lines. They would flit in from the Ivies for a season or two and ruminate on social developments and governmental imperatives and other such lofty fare before returning quickly to their daddies' banks and stock broking houses to amuse people at their cocktail parties where no brown whiskies are served with merry tales of their wild impetuous times as a *ho ho ho* newspaper person. How droll.

But never mind. They didn't do much harm, except the getting in the way. That was then.

I did this for several years, wrapped around the improbable time when I was invited to be a graduate student in journalism at the wonderful University of Texas. Likely the Hook 'Em Horns crowd had confused me with someone else in giving me a scholarship, but I never wised them up and took happy advantage of a year in an amazing center of learning, spirit, beauty and football – to list the local priorities in the reverse order. Academically, it was pretty much a flop, so many distractions crisping the air such as the playing out of the battle for civil rights – where heroes as bold as anyone in formal uniform battled America itself a century after Emancipation to have the right to vote, to live where they pleased, to go to proper schools, to eat at the same lunch counter as anyone else, to pee where they wanted just like anyone else; yet so much of America begrudged them that simple justice that they had to go out and fight and be maimed and killed by Americans to finally get it. Distracting, too, was the growing war way over there in someplace called Vietnam. But the University of Texas experience opened my wondering eyes to a whole new part of the land that I had only imagined from the movies. Scholarship done, I went back to the Globe for a few months more and waited for the Army to reel me in since they had already commissioned me as an officer and might be presumed to have some use for even me. And, when they finally whistled for me to show up, it set the date some six or seven months off, alerting me to likely duty in "Southeast Asia." I sold pretty much everything I owned and went off to Ireland in the meantime, rattling around my shamrock-shaped roots and the pubs of my ancestors, writing occasional columns and book reviews for the Dublin papers to have money to eat. I nearly starved. But I wouldn't have traded the experience for free steaks at the Shelbourne or the Gresham, hotels which had broad-shouldered men in foppy uniforms at the door precisely to keep out such as me. I came home with exactly one dollar in my wallet.

Now, there's plenty of newspapering in all that but not a lot that would precisely prepare me for the challenges of helping run an English-language newspaper in Bangkok, Thailand.

But, then again, how big a deal could that be, running an English-language newspaper in Bangkok, Thailand?

Well, actually it was something of a rather big deal.

TYPICALLY, A FILE FROM A THAI REPORTER would launch something like: "The sun rose at 6:36 a.m. with the wind from the west slightly heavy with moisture, something common to the season, although many can recall earlier seasons when the monsoon winds were surprisingly dry often allowing for grit and ash from the annual rice paddy stubble fires to travel far distances. Mr. Piphob Veralamphoon arose shortly after dawn, washed, brushed his teeth and had breakfast, the traditional broken rice porridge with pork curry with a touch of shredded ginger prepared the evening before. Mr. Piphob noticed that he needed to buy more salt at the market and made a note to do so on his list for the day. Breakfast done, the dishes washed, he took a shower, shaved, with his right hand, chin first, then upper lip, combed his hair and got dressed, putting on finally a pair of brown slacks and a white shirt the housemaid had ironed earlier in the week when he prepared his wardrobe for the office, days in advance, the way he usually did when his wife, Durudee, was away, as now, visiting her parents in Kanchanaburi. He had hung each shirt in a small wardrobe in sequence to the workweek, a practice he had learned from his father, who had worked as a dispatcher at the ministry of transportation's Petchaburi substation No. 4A. Outside his home, he walked the twenty-nine steps east by southeast necessary to reach the bus stop where he awaited the arrival of the No. 7 Soi Ranong bus, a yellow and chrome-covered Nissan Empira with a 348 horsepower diesel engine loosely calibrated to 7 mm of the minimum standard for exhaust impellents as defined by the parliament in legislation proposed by Mr. Seehanat Yennakart of Khon Kaen province who was elected to a third term last November, defeating a surprising challenge from the New Dawn Party candidate, Miss Thida Tantraphol, who was the second cousin to the district's former Officer for Agricultural Affairs ..."

The account would wanderingly chronicle Mr. Phiphob's passage to work, describing carefully who else was on the bus and what they were wearing and what intersections they were delayed at and what the doorman at the office building himself had prepared for his lunch, what the state of repair was of the paint on the walls and the various reflections that could usually be seen caught in west-facing windows .... endlessly rattling on in this manner for meandering page after excruciating page before noting, rather incidentally, that Mr. Piphob quietly walked into the men's room and fired a small howitzer into the ceiling rather startling Mr. Veraphol Michareestabun in the second stall from the window and the entire staff of the Quaker Star Import Agency upstairs while bringing down several square meters of plaster, a dozen lighting fixtures and a three-drawer file cabinet in which had been put, meticulously cataloged, financial reports and employee time sheets and ...

This is precisely the way my wife tells stories, too, where a tale begins with all the richness of a full-breasted, many masted frigate under heavy sail boldly coursing out from the busy dock, its every spar and mast dotted with detail and texture, each bit of canvas and flag flapping in the breeze of shadings and sunlight of background, horns a-tooting and the gulls a-cawing and the people on the shore casting their caps into the sky but which, in mid-harbor, haltingly drifts to turnabouts and misdirections wending this way and that way uneasily indicating, aye aye, that possibly the captain has quite forgotten where the ship or the story is supposed to be headed after all. There is sure charm to this, but it is not always considered the briskest fashion to report the news.

Accordingly, we had a huge staff at the Bangkok World.

We needed people to gather such news and people to make sense of it in English and many others to get it into newspaper shape. We had some twenty reporters, mostly Thai, to cover the news. There were street reporters and sports reporters and business reporters and columnists and so many more. We had some five or more translators, alchemists to convert the Thai into English, and another three or four more rewrite people to reconfigure the buried nugget of Mr. Piphob's howitzer attack into what might pass for journalese to the readers in Bangkok. On top of that, we had a dozen or more copy editors to wrangle the story into the paper, a half-dozen photographers, a few proofreaders and various other department heads, specialists, planners, illustrators, librarians and the like. There are more major league journals today with fewer on the payroll.

It was a grand crew, more varied and colorful than any I had encountered before or ever met together since. Beyond the Thais, there was a Pequod's crew of Chinese and Burmese and Malays, Indians and Pakistanis and the sports editor from Ceylon, as Sri Lanka was then known. There were Brits and Australians, a Netherlander, folks from France, Canada, Ireland, America, New Zealand and Denmark, a fijiian, a filippina, a Swiss and others of no known address.

There were the wonderful Peace Corps workers whose internal filings were lifelong-altered by magnetic work in distant cultures far richer than anything they had ever seen before and who had pale interest in rushing back home again at duty's end. There were drifters and adventurers whom we would hire on Monday and never see again after Thursday. There were those whose pasts were dark, deep secrets, people who would mumble to themselves, twitching more oddly than even the chap in the next desk who whistled a single steady note for long minutes at a time. A very few had had a moment or two's experience in the news game, usually and notably among the Thais, but most were there at least for the fun of it. We paid people nearly nothing, because we had even less than that to pay people with; and the staff worked so very hard and so very beyond any logical expectation that, in time, you barely noticed the Star Wars' saloon of accents and personality styles.

As with most newsrooms everywhere before the highly polished, well-trained and excruciatingly boring wave of youngsters with scads of degrees and scant iotas of street sense took over the business, before the ascendance of bright young beavers who spend more on haberdashery than we spent on automobiles, who fret more about the state of their 401k's than gossip about the richer hanky-panky going on around them in odd pairings-off, back then, in Bangkok as much as in Beantown, an eccentric amalgam of quirky personalities, uneven achievements and cloudy rap sheets somehow blended into an excellently professional workforce producing an incredibly complex newspaper at day's end; and, where the poets and dandies of the ivy must themselves take a year off to recuperate from turning out a mere paragraph or couplet, the newspaper guys would just go out and do the whole thing again tomorrow. And the tomorrow after that, too. No one will ever persuade me there is less talent in even the smallest newsroom than in the most vast, elbow-patched university with all its play-acting and posturing and, only most rarely, actual accomplishment.

The seating plan in the Bangkok World newsroom, a hodge-podge of old battered desks and tables, was as carefully crafted as any ambassador's dinner party chart: you could not sit the Indians near the Pakistanis, this so soon after the wrenching apart of those two partitioned cultures and the ghastly violence that followed and the hatred that continues; the haughty Chinese preferred never to sit near lowly mortals from lesser lands; wild and placid temperaments needed their own spaces; men and women of differing faiths which did not care for the other had to have their leagues of separation. Arguments would burst out and subside again so often that one barely looked up after a time. Vitally, there were great contributors in this menagerie and the whole mass somehow moved together to bring out the daily paper. Against all odds.

The paper was put out from a neat old home in a wonderful city neighborhood in the city's Rajdamnern area, close to the warehouses of authority, but not so close as to have the government come by for coffee – a brew locally prepared with more sweetened condensed milk than actual coffee itself and with which, I think, you could run your motorcycle. As is the unwritten Bangkok requirement, there were glorious temples and monuments in all directions up great broad avenues or narrow, cluttered streets where there'd be 25 shops to the block, noodle shops, engine repair shops, clothing shops, amulet sellers.

Ours was a two-story building that had once been the private home of someone of some stature; no palace or mansion, but large-roomed and comfortable enough for the production of a daily newspaper. The news operation was upstairs; the commercial activities on the ground level. Out back was the composing room with its honeycombs of type, its gritty, inky workshops and just beyond that was the big press that hummed out the daily miracle of the Bangkok World. The place was a hive of motorcycles' coming and going, the rumble of trucks bringing in paper and supplies.

In the small courtyard out front, visitors would need to wriggle through the unending takraw games played by the drivers and messengers idling their time nearby to the hovel maintained by the Indian watchman, who kept his beautiful family in miserable circumstances despite having more wealth than a maharajah from his money-lending operation. It seemed that everyone owed him money, paid back at the crooked, sky-high interest of his rapacious work; yet his children and wife lived as he did in a lean-to affair on the side of the building, barely clean, barely educated, barely sharing in his profits. I always wanted to fire him just for that, but, such was the local culture, I was persuaded that it would have done others more harm than good to have him gone and someone likely even worse in his place. Presiding silently and pleasantly over the scene were the unseeable but serene residents of the building's large spirit house out front, a replica in miniature of a temple full of little ceramic figures, set up, as was everywhere the practice, to house the spirits displaced from the soil and the plants, the grass, trees and bushes, as the building was created. Exactly as is the way at every structure in the land, large or small, the spirit house was provided with respect and attention was paid to the interests of those whose protection and needs were so honored. Every day a small bowl of water was set out along with a bottle of Fanta with a straw, small vases of flowers were arranged with garlands of jasmine blossoms hanging, incense sticks lit and a copy of the Bangkok World provided for the spirits to keep up with the day's events. It is a beautiful custom, the spirit house.

When I joined the paper the spirits were accustomed to reading a two-section morning edition with a slim, neat magazine on Sunday set out in the awkward design compelled by ancient practices and equipment, pretty basic skills and only slight resources. A lot of that would change over time as we ginned up more supplements and additions, sharpened the presentation, and new ownership brought in new equipment. But what remained, always, was a sense of pride and professionalism at an endeavor vigorously played, if not always successful by the financial standards that math-addled commerce requires of any such enterprise.

We covered some of the news such as we calculated was of interest to the English-speaking community of Thailand; we relayed strong samplings of international news, sports, business and features; we heightened the neck-imperiling commentary of local and regional and international currents; we sought to entertain and inform and to be helpful. We did what newspapers do.

What we did not have for very long, sad to say, was Sacha Casella as editor of the paper. I had barely enough time to build, from scratch, a wardrobe suitable for a civilian job of such stature, managing editor, before it happened that I'd need a fashion upgrade as Sacha was leaving – and I'd be taking over everything from him.

It varies widely from newsroom to newsroom, of course, but in most newspapers the job of the managing editor is to manage the editing, to run the news operation on its daily basis, guiding the coverage, supervising the process, enforcing the rules, setting a tone and texture that would carry forth into the paper itself. It's the inside guy role. The assignment of the editor in chief is most often to develop or inflict the paper's overall policy and theme, represent the institution in the community, stare down its critics, be its face, work with her or his owners, deputies and staff on policy and vision. So often, it's the outside guy role. At the Bangkok World the distinguishing lines were hardly so crisp, because everyone did everything all at once to help; but the essential distinctions persisted.

Sacha was exactly built for this division, bringing texture and talent to the mix. I was assigned the nuts and bolts while he took on the course-charting. He was smart, wise to the sweeping complexities of history in the region. As a reporter and observer of the sad situation in Indochina and all of Southeast Asia, he had the strongest sense of how badly things were going in the huge war bloodily scorching the area – and inflaming the world with it. A man of subtleties and shadings himself, he was keenly aware of such in others, and was archly distrustful of the straight-line thinking that had lead to the war in the first place and which had been ever-expanding it since. He had little energy for gauzing over the slips of fools or the blunders of despots. Not directly confrontational, his views were crisp and sharp-edged, caustic, and he was comfortable in explaining them and in believing that others were open to the richness of a vigorous dialogue. Quite often they were not. His views were of the European left, and most often those whom his views affected were not. He saw things – principally the war – in a way that those in power around him most certainly did not.

He was shown the door in a typically Thailand way. It is said that in the early days of the one-after-another military dictatorships if one lesser officer decided to overthrow the ruling general there would seldom be troops in the street so much as the junior despot-wannabe would telephone his senior and instruct him to come to his office. No bluffing allowed. The senior fellow, gauging the situation, would head for the hills with his suitcases of gold ingots and the new guy would be in charge until his own phone began ringing. Very civilized, you could think.

There were no distinct fingerprints around Sacha's departure, no Sherlock Holmes clues to be painstakingly found, no witnesses; but he was just as gone as if the great military machine around him had blasted him to smithereens. The Thai government quietly invited him to leave, with the understanding that, if he didn't, he would have no visa, and if he had no visa and was still there, why, there was nothing else to be done but apply the hammers of hell to his poor head, him being a visa-offender and all.

Not necessarily aimed only at Westerners who might want to barge into Thailand for extended times, the Thais had a rigid visa system more specifically designed to keep neighboring Southeast Asians or the multitudinous Chinese from flooding the place. To live and work there a visitor needs a resident visa, as is common enough in most lands. A few people, in time, could be awarded long-term, nearly permanent visas but these were hard to come by. Ultimately I received one, but my wife for a time was required to leave the country every three or six months and return again exactly like the tourist I was when I first arrived there myself. It was more than an annoyance because it was expensive and time-consuming, and to be caught with the wrong visa or one that has expired was a serious matter. Regularly, foreign members of our staff would take the night train to Vientiane, toe-tap in Laos, and take the same train right back again to Bangkok. If you had a visa, all was well. Without one, you were at the mercy of events, personalities and the iron whims of Thai authority.

Sacha was called in by the bosses, literally weeks after I joined the paper, and was told that the government didn't like him and was pulling his visa and very likely, almost assuredly, would harass and maybe arrest him after. He was totally convinced that the Americans were behind this, his perspective on events being so offensive to them. Myself, I was told that the Thais were behind the thing, his perspective on events being so offensive to them. Others spun the event into all sorts of high drama machinations involving Ital-Thai, the French, the Swiss, that the owners themselves had opened up a trap door underneath him, that the authorities on the planet Jupiter were somehow engaged along with whatever other agents one wanted to include in the dramatis personae in the drama of Sacha's sad status. Less fatally, it was the Jim Thompson disappearance once more. Here one minute, gone the next. But where ever it came from, he had to leave; and leave nearly immediately. So it was that Alessandro Casella moved on, leaving us his beautiful, chestnut-haired but perpetually cranky Burmese cat, Meo, and his assignment as Editor of the Bangkok World.

The odd thing was that Sacha was no great disrupter of things at all. He had intelligent, strong views, breezily shared, to be sure, but he was not reckless or incendiary. He wrote very few editorials, which might have provided some paper trail for those weaving a noose on his reign as editor since his approach might even be somewhat relaxed for daily newspapering of that order. His idea, he assured me, was that editorials should not just be quick reflections of the moment's attitudes but, instead, each deeply-researched and carefully constructed, vetted, aired out to dry, and allowed to temper and ripen like wine. A grand view – for a monthly magazine, maybe – but that was his approach and it hardly created a climate of contention, except to the degree that when he did write something, he usually knew what he was talking about. There's danger a-plenty in that.

Probably I only flatter myself to consider that anyone had even bothered to forecast the consequences of my replacing Sacha and what my views might be on the same principal issues that ultimately might have so imperiled him. Likely there was some small sense that being an American, fresh from the ranks of the military at that, surely I had a somewhat better running start on being in tune with the swelling tides of the moment and with the heavy hands directing those tides. Well, as they say, you can't win 'em all.

Slam.

SOMEWHERE IN THE QUIET corners of the Bangkok World a door would slam. While others might be startled, sometimes I would just sigh. It meant the monks.

The Thai and Buddhist cultures are genuinely beautiful gifts, great clouds of reverence and patient, uplifting spirit, an inextricably en-twined calm easing aside the scratchiness of the heavy life everywhere around, or at least making it so much more bearable to those allowed the much longer view of the instant's challenges. They are a peaceful people, the Thais, moving through the day with intelligence, faith, defining smiles and a sense of peace not easily toppled by the elbows-out bullies of the world who would try to make them into something they choose not to be. Their faith and their king are the ocean buoying up the Thai people in so many vital aspects of their daily and spiritual life. While there are a few shriveled hearts elsewhere who would criticize Thailand's immensely respected Thai monarch, who has guided the nation for so long for, well, being a king and not a grocery store manager or something else, for his people the very, very long-reigning King Bhumipol, Rama IX, has been an inspiration, an authority and a star to sail by, beloved beyond Western understanding, honored, revered. The amazing presence of King Bhumibol Adulyadej, Phra Bat Somdet Phra Poramintharamaha Bhumibol Adulyadej Mahitalathibet Ramathibodi Chakkrinaruebodin Sayamminthrathirat Borommanatbophit, as is written in the most formal royal circles, inarguably has brought pride and stability to a society that could see others in wild disarray everywhere else around it. Everywhere. All across Asia, and most everywhere else too, turmoil and topplings might be ferociously commonplace, but in Thailand there was a cultural steadiness that was and is so deeply rooted in the palace and the temple. A great man and a great gift to his people.

Thailand's Theravada Buddhism is the very air in which all things Thai float. It is everywhere in its hospitable, calming ease. Rich with the wisdom of the Buddha, heightened and seasoned with bits of Khmer and Indian Hinduism and folk energy and spirited mythology, it guides the Thai society from dawn to dusk, from dusk to dawn. It is there in the minds, the hearts, the flowers, the architecture, the history, the vision of life and society all together. It is Thailand's greatest wealth. It is no small thing that so few Buddhist peoples launch holy wars, while the religious passions of so many other faiths are so quick to wreak horror and pain on those who might believe things of the spirit differently. To have even the quickest impression or understanding of the Thai people it is necessary to respect the role of king and of Buddhism. Appreciating it, you have to welcome it as an admirable thing entirely.

That said, there were times when a door might slam in the distance and where a little less of the faith might have helped get the paper out on time.

Doors and shutters sometimes will slam shut in open air places in the tropics where winds swirl and steadily bring in the important rains, cooling and fruitful. With so many open windows, the breezes will cause papers to take wing, sun-spangled dust flakes to float often catching the sunlight to appear as diamond dust in the air – and idle doors to close with a slam. It would happen, though, that sometimes when the door closed with no one in sight to have closed it, some of the Thai staff would have the idea that the spirit of Darrel Berrigan was afoot. Why exactly it was thought that it was the murdered founding editor prowling the Bangkok World rather than, say, a particularly active chingchok was not for me ever to know: If the folks believed it, they believed it. And it was time to call in the monks.

Always respectful, of course, of the faith that threaded together the Thai staff's essence, we would honor their anxiety and agree to bring in those to bless away disturbances in the premises. At precisely the best time, a distinguished monk or two would arrive and pray over the newspaper building. They would run a white string, holy thread or *as sai sin*, around the walls and sprinkle the facility and its workers with blessed water, wafted over us from a brass bowl with a little whisk broom or leafy branches. The senior monk would place flowers in selected spots and make lovely little designs of as many as nine tiny spots and whirls in white paste at exact places – doorways in particular. And upon the forehead of the editor of the paper as well, although often with only three dots for such an unworthy canvas. It is a lovely ceremony and it must have worked as we never did suffer much discomfort from the spectral wanderings of Darrel Berrigan for a while after. Whether he was on the prowl, annoyed at our coverage of the city pothole situation or our efforts to diminish the typographical errors that punctuated his own reign, we don't know; but I am sure that the grand editors at the Washington Post or New York Times never had the luck to be so blessed, or anointed and dotted, as their own newsrooms were so spiritually disinfected. Well, that's their loss.

We respected this, of course, because we were far more likely to be wrong in not honoring it. We worked hard at trying to do what we hoped was the right thing, when we imagined we might actually know what that might be. It is easy enough to know what you already know. The challenge, early on and always, was learning what I didn't know. And there was plenty of that.

After Sacha Casella left, I suddenly became editor of the paper – and publisher, too. I don't particularly remember anyone asking me if I wanted either job so much as it was just presumed that I'd do it. The Thai military government pointedly licensed publishers and editors, sometimes an extensive process, but that went through pretty smoothly, although it is easy to imagine that the wheels may have been greased for this, as they were for just about everything else where considerations were expected for an official's troubles, or for merely doing the job he is already paid to do. The two English-language newspapers, with our small circulations and limited reach, were not exactly high priority affairs in the thinking of the Thai government, which jingled with the brass and medals of its many generals, admirals and strongmen. The Ministry of Foreign Affairs took us far more seriously than did the rest of the regime, anticipating that our reporting and commentary especially reached the decision-making official, commercial and expatriate community, and we were lightly assumed to have more voice than was likely the case. We never much tried to disabuse them of their idea that we had more clout than we actually had.

Bangkok's Thai newspaper scene could be a Wild West affair with dozens of zippy daily papers, some reflecting factions deep within the political and power structures, some serious, and most others amazingly sensational. There were papers that represented the various military services, the leading – if often officially undefined – political parties, commercial interests and the social strata. Most often the That newspapers were printed on paper as wide as a road map with long headlines that could be trumpeting some huge news event or, indistinguishably, the mild hanky-panky of a television personality or movie star. As in most places, the readers knew what to expect in the politics of their own paper and despised and loathed the politics in the paper next to it. The politicians would duke it out and the readers might be growling at each other, but the reporters themselves were all in the same universal fraternity and seemed to enjoy their work and friendships tremendously. There were papers with circulations in the deep hundreds of thousands and others that barely beat out the two tiny English-language newspapers, the World and the Post. There was a wonderful chorus of voices and, with the exception of a few lofty social giants editing a few of them, newspaper people in Bangkok were not always much better considered there than their counterparts in Boston or New Orleans. It was not dull.

With Sacha gone and me so new to the job, I barely knew a soul at the paper but it was pretty much a friendly and forgiving crowd. Almost as it was in the Army, people would afford me the benefit of some doubt based on the position I held rather than any particular qualities that I brought to the job itself. The Thai staff, whatever was in their hearts, offered me respect as editor; the foreign staff, like newspaper people anywhere, weren't all that ready to afford a boss anything more than begrudging acquiescence to my very existence, one miserly doled out so long as I signed the paychecks.

While the cold eye of the government might well be glaring on the Thai press in particular, there were really only a few rules that everyone took into account. Things would change in a tougher time in sad years to come, when the military battled with Thailand's people more violently, but at this point the generals simply sat at the top, getting richer and more powerful; if folks down below behaved themselves and did not much compete for that money or authority, then the brass was content to let us play unmolested.

The rules? We could never – not ever – run a picture of the king lower on the page than any other picture, the king always enjoying precedence of place. Social custom demanded that no pictures of the dead or maimed could appear – even in war stories or of the daily automobile accidents that mangled the population. You could show the crumpled machines of war or traffic, but not the victims. It was simply not respectful. It was absolutely understood that we would never even consider running stories critical of the king or Buddhism. That was pretty much up front and everyone knew it – even me. Less up front was the sense that there were any number of important toes, constantly shifting toes at that, that could be stepped on in the complex politics and diplomacy of the moment, and if anyone had a clue as to how to keep a precise toe-list of who was up and who was not at a given moment, they never shared it with me. Those toes were most often inside combat boots, which could deliver a sharp kick. Sometimes. Sometimes, otherwise, you seemingly could write up the hijinks of officials – oddly even including the prime minister – but had to be very careful indeed not to get the minister of the interior mad at you or, worse, the top police generals, a particularly fearful crowd. Even the sprightly Thai papers knew where to draw the line in their spirited attack on one another's patrons and foes.

We covered Bangkok news mostly, or at least published what news we gathered. A stranger entirely to the town, I had no particular idea about what else might be going on than what the reporters were coming back with. But we had good assignment editors who did know, who dispatched the reporters to the crashes, fires, press conferences and the howitzers going off under the Quaker Star Import Agency. We could help assure that what was published was written and edited well. We covered some crime and wrecks, followed the fortunes of the all-important rice crops, monitored the comings and goings of the mighty as news. The paper when I first got there ran from twelve to eighteen pages a day, in its two sections. There was some advertising, but not a lot. We never really had enough income. The airlines supported us and there were some few ads from the department stores and the movie houses and the hotel restaurants. You could have the paper delivered to your house for a nickel a day, a great bargain.

We had several sports pages a day, more laden with reports of cricket games and rugby matches or soccer contests than made any sense to me; but I appreciated that this was an developing nation and that there was a fascination with such underdeveloped forms of athleticism. We increased the baseball and American football coverage in the wan hope of raising the standards somewhat. The exuberant sports editor would burst into my little glass-walled office a-bubble with excitement to give me the hot news of how Kandurata purely trounced Madhaya Pradesh, nearly agog that someone had reached 50 on 20 occasions but pushed onto three figures just twice while someone else's batting average of 37.55 was below par in the era of big bats, roped in grounds, flat pitches and a dearth of quality fast bowlers; but I nearly had to command him to put in a small account about the World Series which he politely acknowledged as existing but rather in the manner that one might cede that there probably is a Papua New Guinea without imagining that there was a particularly telling reason why there should be. Our business coverage could be pretty good and got better as we increased the focus there. Not that I knew much about high commerce but I understood its obvious importance to a readership – Thai or expatriate – that would use English enough to do business, and read our paper. Fortunately we got lots of advice from the owners who were, indeed, deeply into that world.

There was an excellent photo staff, as there almost always is in newspapering, and a good cadre of freelance art types for design and illustration work when we finally got around to designing and illustrating the paper. We ran comic strips some weeks and months after they'd appeared elsewhere, bought far more cheaply as a result, but nearly impossible to run in any sane sequence because the little coded dates quite often didn't reproduce well enough for our make-up crew to select the one that might logically follow yesterday's. But no one seemed to mind that Mary Worth's adventures might seem to be progressing backwards during a particular week. If we ran the solution to the crossword puzzle in the same month as the puzzle itself it was usually an accident, and if we ran it before we ran the puzzle it solved, well, give us credit for being helpful and prescient. We had an interesting Sunday magazine but, at first, no editorial pages.

Still, for all the typos and the language challenges, the readers got far more than their nickel's worth.

In a season when people now watch 3-D movies on their wrist watches and call down information from the clouds onto their engagement rings with magical efficiency, the idea of putting out a newspaper on typewriters and sheets of actual paper is already akin to making a stone axe or fathoming the recipe for brontosaurus meatballs. The computer and its Internet have turned the already wondrously goofy information world upside down and have opened an era where what happened 20 minutes ago is now ancient history and techniques from the very recent past are almost immediately hoary old relics of museum value only.

How to imagine, then, a room with dozens of typewriters clacking away, with the soft bell ringing just before the end of the typed line? In computer-keyboard offices and what little remains of newsrooms today, all is quiet, hushed, depopulated as when the Black Death hit, and there is so little left of a time when people shouted through the cigarette smoke, when editors actually wore eyeshades – not from the glare from a screen ahead but from incandescent light bulbs above. Ah, yes, my children, reporters really typed on sheets of paper (paper!), and a page was called a "take" and the copy editors might move the story along in paragraph-long spumoni slices, and where each take would be typed out yet again into a linotype machine which actually created, one by one, a line of type, and all would be reassembled in the "chase" from a map drawn by the layout man. Honest. The type was hauled together, backwards and upside down to the floor editor's eye, and a great squashy roller would force the type's crisp characters to carve themselves into a mat from which a lead-heavy casting was made of the entire page which, in turn, was snapped onto the rotary press trickily in sequence where, the presses rolling, an unending river of paper received the inky images that became the newspaper itself. Amazing, eh? That's where I had come in – at the Boston Globe, even at the college paper.

It took more than 450 years for there to be significant advances from Johannes Gutenberg's perfecting of movable type, an invention which changed the world just as entirely as did the Chicxulub asteroid. Ottamar Mergenthaler's typesetting machines, a half-millennium in the coming, were themselves replaced entirely in less than eight decades. Changes now, where things totally amazing at the beginning of this sentence are but quaint and antiquated by the period, replace one another by the week. Offset printing. Photo engraving. Computerized typesetting. Type on paper glued up like wallpaper strips. Electronic editing. Pin point design. Faster than it can be imagined it is outdated by something yet newer.

But that was not at all the way it was the Bangkok World in those early days where the spirit of Gutenberg was more honored than any anticipation of Bill Gates and Steve Jobs. We were tucked snugly between Johannes and Ottamar, and far closer to the former than the latter.

What took place in the backshop at 522 Phrasumaine Road was nearly as museum worthy a craft to me as the one that I knew, before and after, is to today's few remaining newsy scribblers. Today, a story written on a computer screen can pass to the presses themselves with nary a human fingerprint to intrude on the journey. Pages and design appear from the ether, drawn out by a stylus or dancing cursor. Headlines shuffle together like centipedes and photographs emerge from the pixels to leap onto the page in astonishing clarity at a button's push. None of that for us in those early days at the Bangkok World.

Our writers, back in an age when not a one of us would be considered socially respectable enough to appear on television where honest people might see us, worked as hard and harder than any coming along later with all their instant access to the universities and the sources of the galaxy through the Internet. Our people had to go out and find what they could find on their own, actually ask questions in person, rather than by email. The editors there, as daffy as any others today and often proudly more so in an ongoing breed that defies the restraining strictures of mental health unimaginatively insisted upon by other lines of work, brought their unique skills to challenges more daunting than those found now in a moment where the toys do so much of the work. As always, a thousand errors might be caught, while one or two hunker down to survive the scrub-up; and we are more embarrassed by the mistake than proud of the rescues. A story typed in Thai and translated and rewritten in various levels of English would have its facets polished on the fly and hurtle into the paper having passed through so many hands, each capable of leaving yet new scratches on the surface.

The handset type we inherited would wear down, characters losing their shape and sense of identity. The zinc plates or lead castings which became the pictures in the paper would arrive from an outside shop in the wrong shape, or dented from having been dropped as an engraver reached for his sticky rice and mango snack. Ink, having traveled so slowly from far off Europe to meet paper hauled all the way from Canada, would clot up to the consistency of a paving stone. But out came the paper, day after day.

If I had actually known more I might well have had some sense of intimidation at the challenge. But being only young, having wriggled unharmed through various manners of destruction and mayhem, enjoying the surety of the simple-thinking, bedazzled for having married the most nice and most lovely woman in the solar system, and having been awarded the huge assignment of running this very odd endeavor, it all seemed a great lark to me. One that I took very seriously, though.

I was at least smart enough to know that I knew nothing about the high economics of complex commerce, so I leaned heavily on the wiser minds of the office and our leaders. In charge of the business end, I turned often to those who knew that it was not a good thing to have a number in parentheses. Or in red. I understood, too, that the Bangkok World needed more help than I could bring to the challenge alone and I was lucky enough to lure to the game as managing editor one of my oldest friends in the world, Williaml Harting, with whom I had gone to school and worked with at the Boston Globe where he was a genuine editor, tried and true. Being 52.5 weeks older than I was, Bill had accumulated vast experience and gravitas commensurate with his time at actually working for a newspaper, if such duty really qualifies as "work" when there's so much fun in it. Bill and Diane joined us, courageously pulling up their comfortable Massachusetts' stakes to wend their way to the other side of the planet with their three very young daughters, Kara, Jenny and Megan, who performed the miraculous achievement of actually enriching the supply of beauty in that land which seemed in surplus already.

Bill taught us layout developments unseen in the tropics, and the pages began to look like something fresher than ye olde Publick Occurences Both Forreign and Domestick or the Virginia Gazette of yore mode that they lumbered along as before. Bill rallied the copy editors to the virtues of accuracy and precision, investing them with stature and authority where they had prospered with only eccentricity prior. He rewarded with tiny prizes the photographers for especially good work; and they would have followed him into a burning building as a result. He brought to the office a calm and confidence where monsoon winds had been the model, and suggested new ways to chase down stories, write features and present them so that one might actually want to read them. He was an oak where palms took the easy road to sway and be pushed around by the wind.

We didn't have an august editorial board to craft together the paper's lofty commentary. That was my job. I started writing editorials, phasing in to crack wise on the great issues or bright moments of the day. At first, finding my away around the new life, the observation was probably pretty tame, mixing humor and caution as I tried to find a balance and a voice that made sense for a newspaper in Bangkok. Early-on there was plenty of the "a little of this and a little of that," the "reasonable minds can disagree" school of malarkey that usually comes from not knowing enough about what you're talking. I did get better at it, I think, although reasonable minds can disagree. It's not exactly that I somehow learned more so much as how to pass it off as the real stuff; I envisioned it as writing spider webs, seen from the front as neatly structured and soundly wired together but seen from another angle, to the side, as somewhat slim. Nearly every day, though, I met with and interviewed as many diplomats and officials who would talk with me, building up, in crash-course fashion, some familiarity with significant issues and developments – enough, anyway, to get me to the end of the commentary.

Quickly and inevitably the editorials turned to the war, easing from near wishful thinking about progress being distantly possible there to the almost inexorable judgment that things were going very badly indeed and that too many people were dying as a result. It was, of course, the major matter of the day, one which entangled Thailand deeper and deeper with policies that seemed impossible to succeed. As the war only grew and grew, expanding openly into Laos and Cambodia, my views became sharper and sharper but, at that, were but pale sparks compared to the very ugly reality unfolding with such consequence all around us.

I would do little prose poems to the beauties of Thai life or let fly some pot-shot at obscure developments that no one particularly was interested in – giving me the editorialist's aura of faux, pipe-smelling wisdom on matters that no one can challenge because no one both-ers to know or care enough about the subject to notice the sleight of logical hand involved. I would dance around China – then in its mauling Cultural Revolution mess but inescapably the master of the land, no matter what the supporters of Taiwan might say in claiming their moon to be the planet itself. I wrote a lot about the Mideast, too, where other wars had raged, were raging at most given moments or were always on the edge of raging yet again. I was young and foolish and actually believed back then that the leaders of the Mideast surely must want peace; I was wrong, of course. Asia's interest were sharply focused on Vietnam but the intertwined passions of the Middle East, the Big Power rivalries at play, the essential justices and injustices facing the peoples there had echoes everywhere. I saw it pretty much in black and white terms, pretty much always favoring Israel in its struggles against implacable enemies in a place so blessed and cursed.

(But I was to learn that there can be a some grays amid the black and whites, that things were seldom so crisply clear as they seemed. Once on a trip to cover a conference in Djakarta, with the world's largest Muslim population unrelentingly and exuberantly hostile to Israel, I ran into a man at my hotel bar. An Israeli businessman. "What are you doing here?" I asked, surprised, in a place where Israel's business could expected to be somewhat slow. "Well, Indonesia has broken with the Soviet Union," he said. "They were armed by the Soviets and now they have no access to replacement parts. We have a desert full of destroyed Soviet tanks and Soviet weapons from the wars. There's business to be done." An interesting place, the world.)

NOT THAT ANY OF MY VIEWS WERE necessarily brilliant but sometimes the clumsy printing process – and we folks running it – made even more of a muddle than usual. Page seven might somehow run between pages eleven and twelve, sports news might find itself rubbing cricket cheeks with shipping page jowls in the business section. Typographical innovations – such as strange inadvertent spellings, e.e.cummings' capitalizations and missing verbs – leaped into print where none whatever was planned. Planned? Once, after some now disremembered diplomatic assault in the unending campaign against the Jewish state's very right to exist at all, I wrote something pointing out the obvious even to the hate-blinded, that Israel is there for good, like it or not, that it has every right to exist and to wish it away was as foolish as trying to use violence to make it go away on a people quite ready and quite justified to hand you your hat. Something like that. I had the bright idea to use as a headline the near-word-game label:

Israel

Is Real

Clever fellow, me. But this headline was seen as likely wrong by someone down the production line or deemed surely inelegant by one of the proofreaders who blithely changed it instead to read simply:

Israel

Israel

Now that didn't seem to make much sense to me, but it had jumped into print because there was no line of defense behind the errant proofreaders unless we hired other proofreaders to come in behind the first proofreaders which would likely require yet another squad of proofreaders to fix the work of the earlier ones, an Escher-prospect like the man with inordinate fear of the alarm clock's failing who sets out another one in case the first should fail to go off, but then worries that there's as much risk that the backup might fail as there was that the first wouldn't work and winds up a third and then needs a fourth and a fifth until when they all do go off in the morning it is the sound that rattled poor old Quasimodo up in his belfry. It ended up being printed as a correct-enough typo, but somewhere in the odd underemployed world of diplomats and others, I came to be told, the headline sparked knitted-browed chitchat at an embassy lunch where someone sagely believed that I was subtly citing an old British hymn, "Israel, Israel, God is Calling" (of which I had never once heard) while some others, no admirers at all of the Jewish state, found reason to think that I was somehow admonishing Israel. Few seemed to have spared the time to read the editorial itself, apparently. I took the credit for the subtlety figuring that since I'd always get plenty of blame that I didn't always deserve, the rare bit of even misplaced acknowledgment was only fair.

Likely the microscope-peepers wouldn't believe it, but there was more of that to our game than they'd imagined. Once I went out of town for a few days and came back to discover that, grandly, someone had written an editorial that changed entirely the paper's carefully crafted editorial policy on One China versus Two Chinas, which I had been incrementally budging along bit by small bit: a huge issue, with sharp-toothed consequences to the Thais, too, the paper's policy was turned entirely on its head while I was gone and without anyone's asking me at all, landing us with a sudden thud where I cautiously anticipated it arriving a long ways off from then. Once more it was subject of knit-browed discussion as to whether the Bangkok World was significantly reflecting – or anticipating – how the Thai government would be or should be moving in this archly delicate matter and, thus, how wise or foolish as we were, or whether the significant editorial change foreshadowed this or that internal battling among the generals or ... Ah well.

There were more quirks, for which we charged nothing extra, than people guessed, those who imagined that their nickel's worth of newspaper was all done to odd but high intent or design. We were more than capable of making our own blunders and hardly needed anyone else to superimpose deeper meanings into them. Opening the paper so often was an adventure, even for those putting it out. Once, I had received a news item from a local company of some interest so I wrote a note on the top saying to the business desk editor, "Sauna, please put this in the Local Business column when there's room. Thanks, DEH," and I soon saw that heading the next installment of the local business column was the sentence: "Sauna, please put this in the Local Business column when there's room. Thanks, DEH."

Another time I was working away when a pleasant young Thai fellow came into my office and proceeded to talk away with great energy, politeness and enthusiasm. He seemed very nice even though I had no idea at all what he was saying because his tiny bit of English was as mangled and accented as if I were speaking to him in my own paltry, mangled and badly accented Thai. But on and on he went. I heard him out, we smiled at one another and that was that. Except that a few days later I received a card in the mail inviting me to a showing at a small art gallery "hosted by Denis Horgan, Distinguished Editor of the Bangkok World and featuring many paintings of naked ladies."

As I tried to crank back down my startled eyebrows and work up a fiery threat to these mountebanks and their naked ladies, what do I see but that the very same announcement was printed right there in the paper of which I was the Distinguished Editor, the Features staff having gotten the invitation in the mail first and assuming that it was all legit and that my standing interest in naked ladies likely verified its authenticity. Who could doubt it? As it happened, the miscommunication was further distracted upwards by imperfect translation, too, as the paintings I discovered when we went over to the gallery to kick the furniture around were not at all of naked ladies but, instead, were rather good renderings of Thai life, flowers and vistas, in both traditional and modern styles. Suddenly a patron of the arts, I showed up at the reception to warm appreciation of the young artists, exactly as if I deserved it.

The fact that, despite taking lessons and living within the community, I spoke so little Thai is entirely my own fault, no matter the consequences. I tried so hard to master the thing but could never get much beyond baby talk. I had the basic expressions and politenesses and I did try to get down pat the smile which underlies all Thai communication. But it barely worked. Thai is a tonal language with five separate sound paths along which a word could idly venture, achieving a different meaning entirely in a rising tone rather than a low one, a steady tone or a falling away one. If you said the word "silk" wrong you could be saying "tiger" instead, for example. The Irish believe, "You can't teach an old dog a new bark," but I wasn't even an old dog. I had studied languages in school – French, German, Latin and Russian – but none would work when I most needed them. Called on to use a bit of French, a German word would rise out of the swamp instead. Traveling in Russia, suddenly it was the Thai that had avoided me in Bangkok that forced itself to the fore. Needing a number to hire a taxi, say, I would be like a frazzled mother going down the list of her many children's names to snap at an unruly tot, wearing out the coconut starting at "one" and work my way up to the digit I needed.

Pat had better skills than I and worked the Thai language so much more successfully, although she could fall victim to its pitfalls, too. Once when she was returning home from a Thai lesson and *tuk-tukking* along in a samlor cab she noticed that there were water buffalo in a nearby field. Well, now. She had learned the word for water buffalo in her lesson that day, and brightly shared with the driver her appreciation of the impressive size of Thai buffalo and how attractive they were and how much she admired them. This inspired eye-rolling and uncomfortable brow-wriggling from the driver. A Thai friend afterwards explained it away by noting that the word for "buffalo" and the word for "penis" are the same, except for a slight difference in tone.

Another time I was interrupted from my office reveries by a crisp Thai police officer, a lieutenant colonel I saw by his shoulder pips, who marched in on me and delivered what I took to be a firm rebuke to something in the paper as he repeatedly tapped a rolled up copy of the World with his knuckles while lecturing me in unmistakably sharp – but polite – terms. He paced around as he talked, relaying his official offense, recounting surely the wrongheadedness of what so bothered him and his superiors, clearly sharpening his arguments in increasingly precise and lengthy detail. As I nodded and tilted my head this way and that as he ranted away, he seemed relieved that I gave him no argument at all and soon enough he ran out of official steam and we parted with friendly smiles. I had no idea on earth what he was talking about and hoped that it had nothing to do with naked ladies.

Fortunately for me – and the prospects of an English-language newspaper – the use of English was widespread and growing in Thailand. It never seemed quite right that the Thais were the ones to make the extra effort to speak someone else's language and in their own land. There were some expatriates who did not seem to make even the slightest effort to learn the local language but heaven knows that I tried. What I learned, instead, that would carry me through travels in so many odd quarters of the globe, is that the even clumsy trying and the courtesy of smiling and apologizing are universally accepted – while the aloof and haughty who won't make the effort find themselves so often sent to the right when they were asking the way to the left, and get to pay double for their linguistic intransigence.

Storm Clouds

IT IS A GRAVEN COMMANDMENT at every newspaper that I have ever worked for that Thou Shalt Have Spare Columns or Editorials Set Aside in Case of Emergency. As with nearly every other command-ment, I had the best intentions to follow that one but never quite got around to it. Never once did I accumulate spare columns over a long career in the column-writing business. It always seemed to me that should I become ill or get run over by a truck the readers would for-give me being out of the paper for a while. If they didn't, well, being sick or run-over, I already had bigger problems than what they might think of me. As it happens, I never once came up dry over all those decades so I was vindicated as far-sighted in what was merely procras-tination. I never had a spare editorial in the drawer in Bangkok either. In a pinch someone else could come along and do a fill-in editorial if the need arose. When I travelled we would run syndicated columns in the place of the editorials if we had to. There were no rules to break.

Actually, for a few days I did have a spare on hand. It was entitled, "Storm Clouds Over Bangkok" and rather than being any alarum over the many challenges to the region's stability, it was a bit of frost-ing about the incredibly beautiful cloud formations that would pile up each afternoon like vast Himalayas of white surf, fantastically textured and towering. I wrote the rare piece in advance of our son's birth, an event that I imagined would distract me even from opining away yet again on the twigs of the Middle East or currency considerations in the deep Timors.

We ran that editorial on July 28, 1970, the day after the amazing, wondrous, astonishing arrival among us of the most beautiful little boy in the world. Little Denis was born on July 27th, at 8:19 a.m. Well, it was the 27th in Bangkok but it was the night before in distant Boston where so many people waited for the information. Indeed, when I called home to share the grand news and details, there was the usual puzzling over how I could cite an instant that had not yet occurred there on their clocks and calendars. Bangkok, of course, is very far away and considerably ahead of the American timepieces as a result. There is no particular concern about that as Denis celebrates his birthday on the 27th because it was on the 27th that he was born where he was born. There would be quirks otherwise – such as how the Western world says that Neil Armstrong walked on the moon just after midday on July 20, 1969, but it was most surely July 21st in Bangkok when the unearthly stroll took place; I remember it so well, as we were taking the news and picture after midnight from the television to get it into the next morning's Bangkok World. The wire services were just enough moments behind as to make the television our resource as we just barely made our deadlines. On July 21st. The world is a big thing and Bangkok is on the other side of it. But the clock is the clock and wee Denis was born at 8:19 a.m. On time.

If Moonwalker Armstrong's stroll would be the more widely remembered event of the two to so many others with more trifling senses of importance, Denis' arrival was for us the far-more significant universe-brightening happening – and still is. Possibly there are those who have their first child, or tenth, with nary a wriggle to the eyebrow, so cool and casual is the occasion. They would be strange creatures indeed. That was hardly the way for us then, or with his brothers and the grandchildren since. It was The Most Incredible Event in the History of Time.

More so, after all, because it took place in Bangkok, Thailand.

Getting pregnant was far from a finger-snap so. when it did happen the joy and relief left us nearly breathless. A thousand plans formed for this little sprite's future, for his new life among the lovely Thais, amid the beauty of the land's flowers and culture. Far from "home," home would be where he was, where we were all together, so happily. But then came cautious thunder-in-the-distance concerns about how smoothly might go the birth itself, as the doctor found reason to think that some complications might be hovering behind the satisfactions. Yes, we learned as the moment came very close, there was a need to take special steps to make this birth happen safely to both child and mother. A Caesarean section was necessary. Major surgery. But don't worry.

Don't worry?

If there are dark heads of hair, where ever they are, that could actually ever be made to turn white by anxiety, that news was almost enough to blanch mine. Of course I worried. This is a Third World nation ... How well trained are they for this? ... How good is the equipment, the staff ...?

"Probably you are thinking," the doctor said, " 'This is a Third World nation ... How 'well trained are they for this? ... How good is the equipment, the staff ...?' Ah but your understandable concerns are exactly misplaced. *Because* we are a new society everything here is modern, brand new. *Nothing* is old or outdated. We have no medical schools yet so *all* of our doctors and nurses are educated and trained abroad in the finest places: The United States, England, Europe. ..."

Well, exactly so, I thought, relaxing. That's right, I said to myself, easing. This is the best, the most modern, the most sophisticated ...

"So," continued the doctor, "since we have some small flexibility in scheduling this procedure, I have consulted the astrological tables and have determined that 8:19 a.m. is the auspicious moment for ..."

Astrological tables? Auspicious moments?

Had the monsoon winds funneled all their force to that small space, all those comforting considerations of modern gear and up-to-date medicos wouldn't have flown out the window any quicker. But, no storm clouds over Bangkok, the operation and birth went perfectly, delivering to a hushed world the lovely presence of little Denis Edward Horgan Jr., named, as was more the custom in those days, after his proud father even with whatever confusions it might inspire. ("Denis peed on the nurse," Pat told some hospital-visiting friends at the lovely, flower-mad, open-aired Bangkok Nursing Home, and their eyes reflexively turned to give *me* the dirty look.). Possibly the doctor actually had some other worthy appointment to build around that fine morning but 8:19 a.m. remains a time so happily auspicious to us.

My family back in Boston never could fathom that we lived in a great bustling city full of modern conveniences, alongside and within the exotic charms of the Orient. My father was amazed to hear that there was television and high-end communications as he envisioned us talking on coconuts connected by string, idling away the evening darkness fending off tigers and ferocious orangutans. He was from Boston and, as is the certainty among people from there, he could hardly imagine that there was any need to travel to less civilized climes at all. Why would you? The Comanche began at the Dedham line, in his view. If there was only the buffalo'd frontier beyond Springfield, what manner of primitive locale must we be in?

Of course, we lived quite well in Bangkok on our modest salaries, better than we might anywhere else. Back in my away-in-the-Army days of our marriage, Pat was in an apartment where she enjoyed the company of other young women – Thais, Persians, Europeans – whose husbands worked for the hotels or big firms. I interrupted this revelry by moving in myself when I joined the paper and we shared the place with Sacha Casella's orphaned cat. In time, we rented a small but airy house in a Thai residential area where vendors sold hot food from small wagons and carts, where the little chameleons were joined by their much bigger cousins, the dinosaur-looking tokays and noisy geckos, and where everyone was friendly and welcoming. Without such devices as vacuum cleaners or washing machines, we had a maid – a maid! – who cleaned and later tended to little Denis, becoming so protective of that young pastel sprite that she'd not speak to us for days should we dare to snap at him for sticking his fingers in a electric plug socket or some other dangerous thing. We had a puppy for a time which we named Heather but since the maid could not pronounce Heather correctly it was called flower.

We shopped in local open air markets and ate well, although never quite sure what manner of creature might have surrendered up the "beef," while persuading ourselves that it was surely from only the finest Kobe or other notable steer rather than, say, a wayward and carefully pronounced water buffalo. We enjoyed such amazing fruit – rambutan and mangosteens and custard apple, mango and papaya, longan and pomolo and jackfruit some of which required a degree in physics to open and eat or, in the case of the pricey durian, a nose deadened to the cannibal's pantry smell of the thing. An ordinary apple, when such was rarely available, would cost a dollar apiece and a dollar was a lot back then and there. There were movies to see, although many months after their arrival in theaters in the United

States or Europe, for all the difference that might make. If an American movie ran long, the Thai cinema owners simply cut out an arm's length or more of the film without a care over what it might do to the plot. They rearranged entirely the movie "2001" until it made even less sense than it did before, which is saying something. Why? Who knows? On television shows they dubbed Thai voices onto Western actors and you could end an evening with an aching head trying to figure out what was going on in a drama where everyone sounded incomprehensibly the high-pitched, multi-toned same.

Bicycle powered samlors, little three-wheeled pedal taxis with handle-bells, tinkled up and down the lanes and their bigger and noisier *tuk-tuk* motorized relatives worked the back roads, too. We were decidedly the outsiders there but no one seemed to hold it against us much. So far as we knew. Probably the word was out that I was with the newspaper, but they didn't begrudge us even that. Once – and only once – we'd sent out for sodas and a very young girl brought them to us from the tiny store nearby. Coming into the house and spotting me she dropped to the floor and began to crawl on her elbows and knees across the room to deliver the drinks. I jumped up as if I had stuck my own finger into the electrical socket, startling the poor child almost to tears. Such was their way but it certainly was not my way.

But it was all such fun, being an outsider looking in on this fascinating culture and people. Everywhere there was noise – the sounds of street-playing little bare-bottom children scampering around, the cheery calling-out of neighbors and merchants singing the high merits of the wares or food they carried under light shoulder-yokes, laughter everywhere. I may have been as alien to that child as if I had just landed from Ming the Merciless' planet Mongo, but I was only a newspaper guy enjoying everything mightily.

There were Western restaurants, of course, and department stores, "supermarkets" more like convenience stores than anything particularly super. There were theater performances and concerts galore as the various embassies and cultural centers and ministries brought in fine performances to impress the locals and uplift us expatriated heathens. There were thousands of Westerners and other pioneers working in Bangkok, toiling at big companies, working at the trading houses, the hotels. Like ours, when they money enough, their life was easy if their appreciation of it wasn't always so. You could have the sense that some people too quickly came to imagine that they importantly deserved just this well-tended life by some magic entitlement, and that too many began putting on disdainful airs. The way the gossip mill worked, about half the foreigners were rumored to be spying for someone while the other half were similarly imagined to be spying for the other side. Probably the actual numbers were smaller.

In the great swampy heat, dress was light but not too informal and fashionable wear could be had for a song, bespoke suits and evening dresses for the price of a nice sweater at home. Women actually wore skirts in those distant times, and bright colors. With the war going on so close and so few safe nearby destinations, people who traveled flew far away easily on holidays and vacations. Since you had to get on a plane to go anywhere anyway, you might just as well go someplace even more exotic. Air fares were lower than seems imaginable now and, if you had the time, ticket and money, there were plenty of such destinations around. Getting a flight to Hong Kong or Singapore, Bali, Kuala Lumpur or even Tokyo was a snap and it was nearly as easy to weekend there as in majestic Chiang Mai in the north or the cotton-white beaches to the south. Pat and I went to Cambodia, not to search for Jim Thompson in Peter Hurkos' wild vision, but to see the glories of that wondrous place, this with a war going on but before the excruciating madnesses of Pol Pot's national slaughter soaked it in blood, filled its earth with skulls and bones of the millions murdered. We just got on a plane and went there. If you kept your sense of humor, had a modest income and respect for your hosts, being a foreigner was so easy – even as you were so very, very far from home.

BANGKOK WAS AN ESPECIALLY VIBRANT – and important – place on the diplomatic scene in those turbulent days. Consider the times: It was just twenty years after the great war in the Pacific, just over a decade from the terrible fighting in Korea, the battling of the French in Indochina and the British in Malaya; the simmering still seethed from the awful violence following the Radcliffe Award's wrenching apart of Hindu India and Muslim Pakistan twenty years before, and it was just about contemporary with the Sino-Soviet battles, India's border fighting with China, where the ghastly excesses of the mad Cultural Revolution raged and the groans of its great Mao-made famine still echoed, and of the fierce upheavals of Indonesia – and, of course, the bloodshed and turmoil of the latest destruction in Vietnam raged an hour away. Against all that, Bangkok was calm and steady, peaceful in a measure virtually unknown elsewhere in Asia.

Diplomats and entrepreneurs found in the Thai capital an opportunity to do their special business with flair. It was a place to relax, to study and to be amazed, yes, but, for the commerce people, it was their financial interests that brought them there. There was money to be made as the economy grew into the modern era. For the envoys, there were events and currents to be analyzed in an atmosphere not so riven by conflict and pain that you'd flinch at every car backfire. So much of the world's opposing forces, philosophies, faiths and hopes scraped up against one another in Bangkok, yet the guns remained in the holsters. Thai police and Thai army and Thai navy people might well keep a careful eye on one another but the lauded representatives of India and the Soviet Union and Israel and Arab lands and Pakistan and the United States moved around each other with Noh-play politeness and almost operatic affectations of respect. Any untoward rambunctiousness or scratchy internationalist, argumentative behavior would not simply offend the Thai sensibilities but, more, might upset the great fun there was in the entertainment of diplomatic dining. Possibly unlike their superiors back at the ministries and palaces at home, these folks had their heads on straight.

As the editor of one of the two English-language papers in town and, more importantly, because I was the husband of my wife, Pat, who could brighten up a coal mine, we were regularly invited to elegant formal dinners along the ambassadors' circuit, a busy place in Bangkok where the envoys nearly competed, in their quite civilized way, to be the most gracious and welcoming while keeping their ears wide open to the wide-ranging conversations flowing and as the gossip buoyed along bits of information possibly valuable to higher halls of power. From cocktail parties to formal dinners, we sampled the spirit – and cuisines – of many of the world's fascinating corners. It nearly bankrupted us sustaining a wardrobe for such a whirl as was suddenly opened to us but it was simply so interesting and so informative and so eye-opening, so spirit-expanding.

Maybe the wine did, but the invitations hardly went to our heads. We knew that if we weren't from the newspaper they wouldn't have had us in by the back door. But if they wanted to treat us so well and allow us a seat at their finery and culture, we would be quite pleased to attend, thank you very much, even as I understood that there was more than a bit of play-acting in the effort to seem to take me so seriously. From my Army days I had a sure sense that the mock acceptance of my paltry existence that was directed my way from colonels and others so much higher ranking than me was entirely due to my standing just aft to the general rather than having any laughable connection to any wit or wisdom on my part. I knew that, otherwise, I'd be a worthless enough pup to them, someone to whack with a rolled-up newspaper for the general's abrasions; since he was so far beyond their range, I knew that they'd have loved to put the boots to me instead. But they dared not try it, and pretended that I was their pal. That was fine with me, but I prayed each night for the general's continuing good health knowing that the disgruntled senior officers would turn like wolves upon me otherwise. Who'd blame them?

In Bangkok I wasn't about to get dazzled by experienced representatives of complex and often powerful governments all over the earth showing me a little fine attention. We filled out the diplomatic dance card, that's all. Protocol separated us at the table and it was merrily suspicious how often lovely and bright Pat would always have a neat place of honor near the ambassador's elbow while I was tucked away below the salt; but it was always great fun indeed to dine among the swells. There was a lot to learn, so much to see as these worthies danced around one another in matters small and great, of vital interest and importance – or simply in the great dumb prides of the time.

One lovely Thai evening at a dinner at the Indian ambassador's house, our host, someone we knew well and visited often, the always sparky Dr. P.K. Banerjee, pointed out to the guests with mock caution the spicy nature of the local cuisine, aspiring as it did to pay obeisance to the complex richness of his own but which was, for the moment, more meteoric than nuanced. Particularly he coyly warned of the menace there might be in the small plates of tiny green Thai chilies set out as seasoning in small bowls at the table's center. Leonard Unger, the American ambassador from Central Casting, a wise, handsome and savvy veteran of the region, his having served in Laos before Bangkok, allowed as how, yes, the green *prik kee noo* had a particular bite to be treated with respect, and he reached out and took the tiniest sample to taste. Anatoly Rozanov, the appropriately large Soviet ambassador sitting across from him in whatever was the exquisite protocol of the seating chart, seemed not to notice, as I think I did, that maybe Unger had actually taken up no chilies at all.

The Soviet was not to be outdone by any wimpy American, and he boldly snapped a hefty pinch and popped it into his mouth in the fashion that you might throw a load of hay onto the back of a truck. Unger, deadpanning, again praised just how tasty such a delicacy was, enjoyed in moderation, and again the phantom movement of bits of green from bowl to American lip. Rozanov, with a contemptuous thrust of the jaw, theatrically harvested another large haul and cast it deep into his own Soviet maw.

Now, there are those who wonder at the wisdom of squandering high explosives on an opponent when inflicting Thai chili would have much the same effect at such a lower cost. The Thai chili is two parts lava and three dollops hellfire with a fiery dash of brimstone with scorch & sunburn in the middle. This soon became apparent to the unsuspecting envoy from Moscow, whose superior grin soon began to wriggle like the hands of a Thai dancer, a deepening pink flush climbing up his neck to his cheeks and ears, his eyes awash in tears as the depth charge within began to go off. But even as the American seemed to sample yet another chili, the Soviet felt compelled to continue his internal immolation with yet another depth charge of fire and pain, gasping now and blowing invisible acrid smoke rings.

At the evening's end, Dr. Banerjee held us back in a small side room as the distinguished crowd vanished into the limousine'd night. The last gone, he nearly fell into our arms with tears of laughter rolling down his cheeks. "Did ... you ... see ... that?," he laughed and laughed, free from the poker face compelled by his assignment. "What a pair of ... of ..." My own small sense of diplomacy allowed the sentence to go unfinished. Probably the account of the evening's fireworks didn't make the diplomatic pouch back to Delhi the next morning, but this peppery skirmish in the grander conflict between the great powers would be worth a Cold War laugh had it been shared with headquarters.

OF COURSE THERE WAS CONFRONTATION between the Americans and the Soviets that went well beyond piping hot chilies. There was a war going on all around that was anything but Cold. This was only a decade, more and less, beyond Korea, the Berlin Wall, the harsh occupation of Eastern Europe, cliff's edge Cuba, the crushing of Hungary, the brutal smashing of the Czech Spring, revelations of the extent of the Gulag Archipelago and the true reach of the ghastly Stalinist slaughters. Better that the whole thing could have been concentrated in incendiary spices; but it was not.

I knew from my Army times that the embassy Soviets were like fleas swooping down on the troops from Vietnam briefly allowed to rest and recuperate in the wondrously tawdry Patpong Road and other red hot Bangkok barrooms. The Americans would send in our own intelligence people to monitor the Soviet intelligence agents working on the soldiers for whatever they could gather, presumably panning for detail and disaffection from young men far more interested in diversion and debauchery. The bar owners should have given the spies a discount, adding so much to the business as they did. The Soviet bar-hoppers, of course, spoke very good English. Occasionally invited to events at the Soviet embassy, we would chitchat with young officials there who sometimes unfurled perfect New Jersey accents, southern drawls, even the broad A's of Boston's Beacon Hill, people likely to be prowling Patpong afterwards. So it went.

The Soviets enjoyed a pretty frosty place in otherwise tropical Bangkok. Sponsoring movements that were at work trying to topple the Thai government and the Thai way of life, its ancient faith and beloved monarchy, they were up to enough mischief that the local authorities appropriately gave them the cool eye, openly monitoring the comings and goings at the embassy and being as minimally polite as cautious diplomacy allowed. At the same time, the Thai government, of course, knew well that the Soviets and Chinese and other trouble-makers and their proxies were a significant force that pretty much couldn't be ignored or isolated entirely. It was a careful dance to perform, but they had been doing it well for a long time.

It was everywhere and it was almost hard not to get snagged up in the game. Each year the Soviet embassy formally would sent around some Jack Kennedy-sound-alike to wonder if the Bangkok World would publish an advertising section marking their national holiday commemorating the revolution of 1917, a standard bit of self-congratulation and flag-waving such as we produced for so many other embassies. Each year we would decline politely, knowing that any such a thing would very likely offend the Thai government which would be more mad at us than at the Soviets; besides there were no Soviet companies to advertise in the supplement, commercial enterprise not being a big part of the Communist system. There was nothing but headaches in the prospect of doing such a thing. No thanks.

In early 1970, though, that changed. Almost reflexively, the embassy wondered whether we would publish a special supplement to mark the 100th anniversary of the birth of Vladimir Ilyich Lenin. I'm not exactly sure why it was that I didn't just-as-reflexively decline the opportunity once more; but I began to wonder whether there wasn't a slight chance to do things a little differently.

But not being a fool entirely, I quietly ran the idea by the police

authorities, those grim generals and colonels who controlled so much
– including licensing of editors and publishers of newspapers, and the
newspapers themselves. What do you think, boys? Surprisingly, after
only a brief time, the word came back that, yes, it would be fine for us
to run such a insert – with a few minor restrictions: The section had
to be clearly marked as a product of the Soviet Union; no picture of
Lenin could exceed a certain generous size; and it would be acceptable
to call Lenin a "Communist leader" but not a "world leader." Interesting.

So I went back to the Soviet embassy officials and allowed as how
we might consider it, wringing my hands at the terrible peril such a
courageous step would put me and my newspaper in, how I was risking my neck and career but, *da*, we would do it – and all for merely tri-
ple the rate that we'd turn out such a thing for, say, the Costa Ricans.
They seemed amazed and immediately agreed to everything, making
me kick myself that I hadn't asked for five times the running charge. I
was never much of a businessman. They soon delivered the makings of
the supplement, which we went over with a magnifying glass to make
sure there were no tricks hidden within that would, in fact, imperil me
and my newspaper.

Out came the section and up went the usual howl about how I was
insensitive to Thai interests and the like, with the Foreign Ministry
doing some ritual yapping at me as if we were somehow dim enough to
believe that they weren't a big part of the decision to allow the section
to see the light of the Thai day as part of their own careful diplomatic
choreography. Some of the most staunch anti-Communists railed
against me and the paper, while it was good for several free lunches as
the Americans and others tried to probe how the thing played out to
happen in the first place. The most direct consequence was that I had
to cut back on even the rare social engagements at the Soviet embassy,

for whenever I did show up I would be hauled into the crushing embrace of the chili-scalded ambassador, who thought I was the bravest soul in the entire Asian hemisphere for boldly confronting entrenched opposition to his government and its awful policies. A better consequence is that, months later, I parlayed that bone-breaking goodwill into a visit to the Soviet Union, a trip marked by amazingly adventurous and wild sexual escapades.

Well, not exactly.

Combining a vacation with my parents' visiting Rome, where we worked it out to meet and to have our lovely new baby baptized, I got it into my head that a visit to the Soviet Union would be a grand thing, since I was in the European vicinity after all; it was only 1,500 miles or so away, practically next door. In those days you didn't just drop in on the Soviets and I wondered whether I might have some special timely opportunity open to me because of the Lenin birthday card that would surely wither away from disuse. My new bear-hugging pals were eager to oblige with the Soviet arrangements and the trip came together in a flash.

Now the Soviet Union was a dark, brooding place and, after all, Americans were in a pretty hot conflict with the Communists across Southeast Asia and in unending confrontations large and small everywhere else, so I had a little understandable unease about casually calling in at a place I knew so very little about, and what I did know was hardly comforting. In time, memories fade and old rivalries come to resemble ball games between the Red Sox and Yankees, but the differences between these two forces were very, very real in those days and the stakes being played for were incredibly high, all with enough bloody consequence to make the prudent heart cautious so as to not to make some foolish blunder from not knowing my way around.

I mentioned my planned trip to a friend from the American embassy who suggested that I talk with an official there who had just been reassigned to Bangkok after a tour in Moscow. Yet another "cultural attaché." You would think that there was more culture being exchanged than dollars, bullets and rice, there being so many "cultural attachés" at all the embassies in Bangkok. Oddly, I seldom noticed any cultural attachés at the various cultural events that sprinkled across our calendar. Likely they were busy at other things.

Over lunch, this guy told me that I probably had very little to worry about, so long as I behaved myself. "Look, you're an editor from Bangkok. They think they like you. They'll take good care of you. If you were working in Europe, it might be quite different. Asia they don't care so much about to try to lure you into trouble." He did warn me of some important cautions. "Don't play with money exchanges on the street. That could be a trap. And never buy any black market icons; they're very sensitive about that. Be extremely careful about accepting any letters or documents that someone asks you to carry out of the country; that could get you and others into really deep trouble. And, of course, there's always the question of sex ..."

Sex.

"Yes, it is a pretty common thing for visitors to get lured into sexual situations and then there's suddenly lots of photos and blackmail. Be very, very careful about sex."

Ah, no problem.

Excited but still a bit anxious I finally got on an Aeroflot plane in Copenhagen for the flight to Moscow. Almost to set the tone, I was the sole passenger on the plane. The only one. I had an aisle seat and, after take-off, I slid over the to the window seat to see the world below. A flight attendant quickly told me to return to my own seat. The one to which I was assigned. Okie doke. No fool, I was getting the drift here.

Welcoming me at the Moscow airport was a junior foreign ministry official, Stanislav Mikhailovich Semenev, assigned to guide me around in advance of his own coming assignment to Bangkok, likely as a "cultural attaché." "Ah, Mr. Horgan. I resemble you from your photographs," he said. He didn't much resemble me at all but he did recognize me and I recognized that his English – immeasurably superior to any Russian I might have – was not quite on the level of the crowd working the troops in Bangkok. It seems a bit snippy to make light of the fact that his English was about 80 percent true when my Russian was limited to greetings and reading about half the alphabet. But, I do have to say that he did mangle the language. He was a great companion and guide and translator, who just managed to work a major malapropism or ear-clanker into most sentences. Showing me a gigantic ancient mortar outside the Kremlin he assured me, "It takes big balls to fire this cannon." I agreed. "We will take a left turn here," he would say, turning right. I agreed. Small stuff and he was doing his best, which was a lot better than my best when it came to languages. We took the train to Leningrad, as it then was called. We saw the Hermitage, or perhaps a millionth of that gigantic art-barn. We visited empty churches. Factories. Monuments. "Multi-storied buildings." The Soviets set me up with a hundred interviews, mostly on subjects of little interest to me or my Thai readers. We saw the sights, drank vodka at every stop. He never left my waking side.

But there was never a mention of sex.

One night, though, back in Moscow, he took me to the Bolshoi Theater where we watched essentially a vaudeville show with grand singers and comedians (whose audience-killing jokes were rather lost on me) and dramatic exhortations and jugglers tossing knives and torches to the ceiling. There were dancing and skits. It was all such great fun.

Afterwards, we walked back to my hotel, the cavernous, charmless Rossiya which was about the size of Montpelier, Vermont, passing quite alone in the ocean of darkness, through the vast Red Square. It was so eerie, evocative, spooky. The beautiful onion domes of St. Basil's Cathedral glowed over to our right. Lenin's Tomb, with his unending honor guard, was squatted behind. The monstrously huge, great hunkered-down GUM store was ahead. A truly enormous square, where troops and tanks and rockets paraded by the tens of thousands, totally empty now but for Stanislav and myself, our footfalls clear and sharp in the hollow, haunting night.

After some silence, he said to me, walking, staring directly ahead, "Mr. Horgan. Do you like sex?"

Uh, oh. Here we go. "Well, yes, of course, but I do not want any sex," I said forcefully. "Sex is not for me. Oh, no."

"Ah, but sex in Moscow is *very* good," he said, always staring ahead as we walked walked walked in the dark.

"I'm sure it is, yes, but I must be very clear to you I am not interested in sex. No, no sex for me. None. No."

"Have very beautiful people. Women swinging from the ceiling. Pretty costumes that shine. Animals jumping about ..."

Even as I began to waver and second-think and weigh, hey, what the actual consequences of a little blackmail between friends might be, it slowly dawned on me, trudging along in the Red Square black, that he wasn't talking about sex at all ... but about the *circus.*

We finished our walk in salt mine silence, me brooding over the lost fantasies of women swinging from the ceiling and Stanislav wondering what on earth is wrong with this crazy American who is getting all worked up about not wanting to see the circus.

With basic communication difficulties like that, small wonder the Cold War went on as long as it did.

Years and years later, Pat and I took a trip across Russia, as it reverted to being, riding the wondrously long rails between Siberia and Moscow through a hundred billion birches and the unendingly beautiful countryside with tight little blinking towns nearly lost in the vast landscape. We had come up through China and Mongolia, stayed in a small village at Lake Baikal, and rode the amazingly built steel trail across the seven time zones towards the west, stopping here and there along the way. It was a fascinating adventure, even seeing the terrible graveyards outside Ekaterinburg, where thousands died on the same day, courtesy of the evil Stalin's purges and where people to that day would call at the door of the old KGB headquarters in the city – right there by the statue of the Russian radio pioneer Alexander Stepanovich Popov. ("You think your Macaroni did it, but Popov was the inventor of radio. Not Macaroni, no! It was Popov. Popov!," firmly said our guide, Stanislav's heir apparent, to us.) They would knock, and ask, "What happened to my grandmother, Oya. My uncle, Vassili?" Told to wait, someone would come back and say, "She was shot in 1938. He died on the train east and his body was thrown away." And the door would slam.

There was plenty of time to think on the Trans-Siberian railroad on our trip and obviously plenty to think about. I spotted in a cast-aside Moscow English-language newspaper a small story about a Gallup poll of Russians which asked them what they feared the most in life. The answer? What did they fear? Not war. Not terrorism. No, they feared famine the most. How very interesting, I thought. Likely there are not three people in the entire United States of America who would say "famine." But once someone has experienced famine or dreads famine so much from family history maybe it shapes what powers they'd allow the government to hold, if part of the trade-off was to prevent such a horror again. You might do that or fight less for your liberties than might other peoples whose own fears of government instead cluster around footnotes to tax policy or other slight, bureaucratic infringements.

Back home again later I was talking on the phone with a friend about the trip and mentioned the poll, me waxing away about a huge nation that is so fearful of famine, of all things, above all else. Famine. "What're they afraid of? What's the big deal about that?," she said. "I thought they were tougher than that." Well, they have had some bad times with famine ... "Come on, that seems pretty wimpy ..." We went back and forth like this for several rounds before I tumbled to the fact that what she thought I said was that what the Russian people feared most was *salmon*. You know, they should just step back from the water. Don't go in the boat. Miscommunication about bread and circuses and things Russian seems to follow me about.

Hot Water

IN THE VERY ROUGH AND TUMBLE SPORT of Thai boxing each bout of tumble & rough kicking and butting and punching is preceded by a gentle, balletic moment called Wai Khru Ram Muay where the fighters perform a near-dance of slow-motion pantomime with graceful, flowing kicks and smooth strikes, with lithe weaves and floating dodges, all meant to show the opponent and the world the vast skills that might soon find expression in the explosion of actual violence to follow. It is very pretty, the Ram Muay. No one ever got hurt in the Ram Muay. That comes after.

I still have tucked away in a file an undated memorandum from late 1970 to me from our senior Thai editor, Prasong Wittaya. Long yellowed and faded, it relays a report from Athorn, one of our reporters:

"While covering a sport event at the Royal Bangkok Sport Club about two weeks ago I had a chance to meet Foreign Minister Thanat Khoman and interviewed him on political problems.

"finding out that I represented the Bangkok World, the Minister complained about the way the World presented the news and especially articles ... Col. Thanat said:

" 'Bangkok World is a tool of Nixon's opposition and uses Thailand as an arena to attack the U.S. government which is detrimental to Thai-U.S. rela-

tions. Bangkok World recently also created a situation by publishing false news saying that Burma's General Ne Win was about to die. The Thai embassy in Rangoon was criticized and the incident had marred the Thai-Burmese relations.

" 'In this regard I had summoned the American Ambassador and asked him to advise Mr. Horgan not to do things like this again. Otherwise I will propose to the Police Department to consider deportation of this man from Thailand.' "

There are so many fascinating things in this little memo, a moment in its amber, not the least that our reporter so leisurely waited two full weeks before passing along what someone else a bit more hasty might possibly consider a major tidbit about his newspaper and its boss. Of course, you wouldn't want to rush things, mind you. Will it be any less true tomorrow than today? No, it will not. So why hurry today? There are uncountable tomorrows but only one today, what will we ever find to fill them up? Best to save for then something of so little importance, putting off 'til tomorrow what might only recklessly be done today. But that would be the fashion in which so many things often were done in Thailand, where it was so frequently the easier way to glide around things rather than face them: if the bad stuff went away, well, what was the hurry then to make people uncomfortable?; and if those bad things do land like a ton of water buffaloes, well, so they land, and what would have been gained by worrying about it before? Also, in translating the verbatim account, the always diplomatic, always gracious Prasong had first typed *"consider deportation of this* gentleman *from Thailand"* but weighed his mood-softening translation more accurately and, probably with a sigh, returned to finally render it, *"consider deportation of this* man *from Thailand."* Clearly the minister had not at all referred to me as a "gentleman."

The rest, though, can be clustered under: Isn't Everything A Little Daffy Here?

I was pretty comfortable then and am still so today to be listed on the opposite side of such as Richard Milhous Nixon and, inadvertently but just as surely, the vicious Burmese Junta. I think maybe history has more fully tallied up the merits of my positions and those of, say, Thai Foreign Minister Col. Thanat Khoman on matters Nixon so there's likely not much to reconsider there. By me, anyway.

But how interesting, maybe, that Thanat would feel so aggrieved that I was critical of President Nixon, enough so to call in Nixon's envoy to deliver a sharp threat toward me through him? If, as might be expected, Ambassador Unger himself had felt at all the mosquito bite of my editorial criticism of Nixon's policies toward the war in Vietnam, Laos and Cambodia – there was plenty else to criticize even from so afar but it was the war; it was almost always the war – mightn't Unger have called on Thanat to complain, rather than this other way 'round? What authority exactly did Thanat imagine Unger held over me that it became the ambassador's assignment to haul me into safer port? If the foreign minister thought somehow that Thai-U.S. relations were made queasy by an American editor criticizing an American president's policies in the small local newspaper then how fragile indeed must be Thai-U.S. relations? Not that they needed any particularly logical underpinning, but how might it look, for its 15-second life span, for someone to be deported from Thailand presumably back to the United States for being critical of Richard Milhous Nixon? And wasn't I, at the same moment as being menaced for being anti-American, also being somehow keelhauled as being on the payroll of the American intelligence establishment and what in blazes sort of American spook might I be if I were run out of town for criticizing American policies when there were those who claimed I was likely working on the American dime?

Whatever U.S. cudgel Thanat believed would be used to raise welts atop my poor head for so writing in Thailand, Unger & Co. never once advised me "not to do things like this again." It is hard to imagine a seasoned American diplomat getting stuck on that particular bit of flypaper – even as he might very well wish that there was no such criticism at all of policies that he was there to represent and that he presumably supported. This is not to suggest at all that Unger would ever give me the sly wink on things so important to both of us separately. We did talk often over those times, and he did disagree openly with some of my observations, views that time ultimately proved to be more right than those, say, of Richard Nixon and Thanat Khoman. Unger did advise me collegially that the Thai government wasn't always pleased with me, but there was no scoop in that bit of gossip.

The fact that the "Police Department," which held the license on my work life and comfort, never did get around to deporting me likely suggests that the foreign minister never actually whistled for my ousting: it is hardly conceivable that if Thanat wanted it that the police wouldn't have done it – although, Sacha Casella notwithstanding nor standing at all in Bangkok anymore, there was no great rash of deportations at all in those days, nor other open punishments of the few other local and international journalists who also spoke up and spoke out against a war that was corroding the entire region. In the interests of efficiency and common courtesy, I almost hate to imagine the foreign minister having his version of General Black's analysts puzzling over our media writer Manoj Vudha's work trying to find the heads and tails of my own writing and status: "I tell you there's a code in this! If this man is an American but he speaks against the American war as a tool of Nixon's opponents yet is purported to be in the pocket of the Americans, how can he be both? Or neither? And if a tool of Nixon's foes is getting the western free pass to criticize Nixon's policies then how can the American ambassador influence him to ... what? ... stop? Or increase? So if we fetch the American ambassador to complain about this anti-American who is pro-American and nothing happens, what is the dark message in that? And who in blazes are these Boston Red Sox?" Maybe if I had included the deer shortfall in Lumpini Park, the circle would have been closed.

It's merely footnote territory to note, as well, the "Col. Thanat" in the reporter's memo. Thailand then, and for so much other time as well, was ruled by the military who had long ago taken over the working controls of the constitutional monarchy, gobbling up power and authority and wealth – and to protect itself from scrutiny, progress, honesty and other pesky forces considered debilitating to military dictators everywhere. There was a huge and Gibraltar-like bureaucracy that carefully tended to the running of the country, no matter which junta was on top at any given moment so things got done as the generals and marshals skittered along above. The government was run at the time by field Marshal Thanom Kittikachorn, who seemed likely to topple forward from all the medals on his chest. Mostly, it was full generals who ran the other key parts of the government, themselves bejeweled with baubles and badges.

Of course, Thailand's military happily had pretty much never had to fight anyone at all and that is a good thing as fighting people hurts; but its brassy leaders had seldom used their vast military apparatus against anyone except the Thai people, and one another. They had the small detachment in Vietnam and a well-thought-of unit had fought in Korea in the war there but few if any of the marshals and generals had enough to do with those risky events to warrant decorations – and the self-awarded medals were mostly tinsels of distraction, honors bestowed by one general upon another as if they were really soldiers who might have earned such trinkets instead of the puffed-up popinjays they so much seemed.

Thanat was no general, instead an honorary colonel bearing no stars in that particular galaxy. A very intelligent and dedicated representative of Thailand's vital interests, he required rank of some sort to hold up his head in the military circles for which he provided much-needed brainpower, and cover. So he was designated a colonel. In the Thai press he was called, "Colonel Thanat," as was the custom. But in the English-language press it was "*Mr.* Thanat," that he preferred, thank you very much. Seemingly, he didn't want the even-subtle link with the militarisms, and whenever his colonel moniker would inadvertently slip into our paper, I could expect a quiet call from one of the Foreign Ministry's oleaginous aides suggesting, in uniformly patronizing British-education tones, how it would be so much better to simply refer to the lorded but humble minister as "Mr." rather than by his worthy and important but purely ceremonial military rank. Appreciating the sensitivity, we would "mister" the man thereafter—until, after gnawing on my ankle too much, he would get a dose of the "colonel" in print in petty retaliation. It wasn't much but, after all, it wasn't me threatening to have him bounced from the country. You take your small satisfactions where you can find them.

The foreign minister obviously had a tough job, one he made a bit tougher, maybe, by losing even a second of his time worrying at all about what was appearing in the Bangkok World. His deft brilliance on Thailand's diplomatic behalf hardly clouded the truth that the kingdom might well get a lot more tanks and rifles, helicopters, PX privileges and shoulder-patches from being in the Vietnam war, but that it was risky game altogether – and that Richard M. Nixon would prove to be not the best partner to have embraced. Nor the longest-lasting. As it happened, the Domino Theory that so much of the war-thinking in those days was supposedly built upon proved to be flat wrong an inch beyond the Indochina the French had cruelly cobbled together long earlier. Vietnam did hold sway over poor little Laos and unevenly over Cambodia for a while, but the Vietnamese already had those Dominoes in hand before the Theory was supposed to kick in. Thailand found itself with hostile and scrappy opponents along its long borders with Cambodia and Laos but there was little enough new in that. Thanat's and Thailand's policies of confronting neighbors who were dead-set on paths totally inimical to Thailand's social, economic and religious order made essential sense, more so, frankly, than the Americans' engagement thereabouts. But linking up so forcefully with the American war across Indochina was a far more risky prospect considering that just about anyone who was looking with clear eyes could see that the war was not going well at all.

I remember, in a sunnier moment, the same Dr. Thanat saying, "Why is it that *our* Vietnamese and *our* Lao and *our* Cambodians don't fight as well as *their* Vietnamese and *their* Lao?" Likely, he knew quite well that *their* guys were variously better motivated, tougher, better lead than our allies, and that these qualities counted for more on the jungled battlegrounds than any rightness or wrongness of a cause, even sometimes more than a vast difference in the available machineries of war, wealth and international stature. There is an old saying from an early Texas lawman that remained in my foggy mind from my time studying in the Lone Star state: "No man in the wrong can stand up against a fellow that's in the right and keeps on a-comin'." Right or wrong, the Vietnamese Communists kept on a-comin' in a hard fashion that made quite another fine mess of confident expectations, very high-priced diplomacy and astonishingly destructive military strategy.

I did not at all stop writing about the war. I didn't treat the threat cavalierly – that would have been reckless – but I didn't change what I was doing. I couldn't. It was apparent to me then that the foreign minister's beef with me was not really that I was critical of President Nixon in the Bangkok World but that any criticism of what became

Nixon's war was opening a door to criticism of Thailand's deepening role in it. No one else there at all was making these points. The Thai papers cautiously didn't much examine the war at that point. The Bangkok Post was famously close to the whims and wishes of the foreign ministry. In the United States and Europe and elsewhere it might be common to criticize the Vietnam war, but that was not what happened in the kingdom of Thailand. But even before it became crystal clear from the Pentagon Papers' revealing how the war was crafted and manipulated from the very beginning for the wrong ends and so much more evidence described that the origins of the war were deeply rooted in lies and deceit at horrendous cost, it was widely and sadly understood, considering the costs, that the practice of the war was masked in deception and failed strategies, that there was no doubt that the leadership in Saigon was too flawed and corrupt to warrant the term "leadership" and that the Vietnamese people paid a very, very heavy price for that. Not incidentally, the war was going very badly as well. I would write that.

As it happens, I think that I was mostly pretty careful to focus my editorials on the dim progress and outlook for the war itself, the cold blindness of American policy to the realities on the nearby ground and certainly on the poor quality of the Vietnamese government that so many were getting killed to sustain rather than on the Thai involvement; but surely that was only a slight distinction to Thanat Khoman and the Thai government.

The prospect of being in trouble, even of being deported, was no small thing in that climate. I so loved being in Thailand; I had few options elsewhere; a disruption would likely chew up what little we owned, hurtling me out into a career void that yawned unknowingly ahead. I knew that. How could I not? But how could I not write what needed to be written? What would be the point or value of staying on, just to have the job, if the job's great responsibility to reflect on policies for which thousands were dying every week, was to be muzzled entirely? That may sound very lofty but, really, there simply was no other option that I could see. As events arose, I would write, observe, comment, criticize. No one from any embassy nor from my paper's ownership ever commanded me to take a different tack.

Rather unused to it, criticism and doubt was not welcome in those top Thai government circles – particularly from a foreigner. While the prospect of the foreign minister's calling in the police generals was unsettling, I worked with the sharper sense that there were other matters to worry about from the official quarter than even the concerns of the thin-skinned foreign policy corps.

Tea Money

BEFORE THE GREAT CITY'S SPIDERWEB arteries clogged up with automobiles to where it can now take two hours to go two miles, Bangkok
traffic was marked by Boston-style automotive madness, where cars
would shoot across lanes as if the steering gears had exploded, where
drivers would hurtle down the block at 3-G speed to shriek to a halt
every 50 yards along the way, where cars would take a right turn
from the left lane and a left from the right, where it was expected and
demanded that the slow, the weak-of-will or the too-easily terrified
would get out of the way or suffer the consequences. There were no
rules that anyone minded: ferocity behind the wheel was the virtue,
a survival technique; there was no place at all on the streets for the
timid. No place for me, certainly. And, at that, everything was Ginger
Rogers' dancing-backwards, driven on the left, British-style, a mad bit
of automotive eccentricity that made the passage through a Thai inter-
section or around one of the great roundabouts the inspiration for Ed
Munch's howling painting, or the real-life version from terrified travelers on the streets and byways.

In Cairo they drive like that. In Tehran, too. In the third and
fourth circles of Hell, such is the fiery driving etiquette. People in their
right mind did not dare drive in Bangkok, or, if so, they did not remain in their right mind for long. Most westerners took taxis, where in

those pre-meter days more time was spent melodramatically haggling over the fare than actually traveling to a destination. It was all High Theater with the prospective passenger magnanimously offering to pay a thin dime for a twenty-mile ride while the harried driver would counter with a fare at about the cost of the vehicle itself and each would bemoan the harsh destruction that such a fare as the other's would inflict on the individual, the nation's economy and the grand balance between all things that are good and those which are terrible to behold; after mock tears and general hair-pulling, the driver would reduce his demands to the cost of two motorcycles and a full dinner at the Oriental Hotel and sigh that his family would have to wither even at that; meantime the passenger would counter with an offer matching the price of a small flower but grind the teeth that the ruination of the society would follow for surely such extravagances would offend and topple all senses of value; next the driver would whittle off a few cents here while the traveler would propose adding cash in the thinness of a layer of paint there but would predict poverty unto the seventh son, and back and forth it would go until with eye-rolling and shrugging the middle ground would be reached, such as could have been anticipated at the very beginning except for the vast fun there was in the contest itself.

Or, if possible, maybe you could have a driver. They had a driver for me, the company expecting that it was cheaper to engage someone to drive than to pay for the car's replacement and, less important, the funeral costs after my inevitable wreck.

The newspaper assigned a nice fellow named Preecha to get us through the day. A fine young man, he spoke very little English but needed none to drive so well and so safely. He had our lives in his hands and he never failed to keep up perfectly safe.

Automobiles cost a fortune in Bangkok, the price doubled by

import taxes aimed at revenue-raising and holding down the number of cars. It didn't work. Cars were everywhere and arrived upon the pavements faster than the roads could handle them – or drivers could develop the skills to operate them. No matter. People seemed not to much care that the cost was so high. The poor couldn't afford such a thing no matter the price, and the wealthy and those with commercial interest to get from there to here simply paid what needed to be paid. For my use, the paper had a new Toyota Crown, a smallish four-door sedan that worked just fine for us with Preecha at the wheel.

One day we were rattling along in the traffic, creeping up to a traffic light, when we were ordered over to the side of the street by a young policeman whose assignment it was to wave his arms at the traffic as it passed by, it usually quite ignoring him. Preecha left the car and talked with the policeman for a time and came back and we drove off.

"What's up?" I asked.

Preecha explained, in bits and pieces, that we had been stopped because the police officer noticed that we had an old license plate on our new car. There might be a new plate on an old car but there shouldn't be an old plate on a new automobile. He was suspicious about that, and gave us a ticket for improper paperwork.

As I thought about that I was deeply impressed. Here was a man standing in the city's horrendous heat, swallowing pounds of the under-regulated exhaust grit and other urban pollutions despite the doctor's mask police officers wear on traffic duty, and yet he was attentive and resolute enough to notice an old plate on a new car. Very admirable. Admirable enough that, soon after, I wrote a little note to the police colonel of that part of the city, singing the praises of this sharp-eyed man of his and how the fellow was a tribute to the force, etc., etc.

Shortly thereafter the paper's general manager mentioned in passing that he'd heard the police officer had been punished as a result of my note.

What? I thought I was doing a good thing.

Wrong again. It seems that what had happened on the hot city street that day was that the policeman had, yes, spotted the odd plate and pulled us over. As was the custom, known well to Preecha but less so to me in the back seat, a little bribe would take care of the matter on the spot. The officer pocketed the money. When my note arrived, the policeman got into trouble for not having shared the boodle with his superiors as would be expected. He had broken the corruption code by keeping the tea money for himself entirely.

We tried to track down the offending-offended cop, me figuring, guiltily, that maybe there'd be some place for him and his skills; but we could never find him. Probably he wouldn't have wanted anything to do with the dimwit farangs, outsiders who had cost him his neat job. Likely, too, he couldn't stand the pay cut.

WHEN THE GREAT ROLLS of newsprint would arrive at the port we had already paid the Canadians and the shipper for the freight. But then we would have to pay a little something more to have them unloaded quickly, again to have them placed on trucks, more to have the trucks inventoried and pass through the gates. If the truck needed an inspection sticker, we would pay a little above than the listed price to get one in the same decade as the application. When we bought supplies, we figured there would be fixed prices, and then there would be costs on top of that. A license for a car or an immigration permit would cost a few dollars up front and a few dollars on the sly to make it happen within the lifetime of the person making the request. Bit by bit, it might never much but, over time, it did add up. I never understood the accounting system for such off-the-books levies but somehow it was massaged through the system, likely with a dose of tea money of its own somewhere along the line.

Repeatedly, around the world, it would be revealed that some huge airline had paid millions and millions in bribes and sweeteners to high officials for sales or landing rights, that tons of oil company money was diverted to some tinpot generalissimo or another, yet the true constant grind of corruption is most felt at the lowest levels of the society. The airline, the airplane manufacturer, the burping oil bosses, the businesses at every level were going to pass that cost along. The infection from the small scratch might show up six levels down the line, but show up it would. That would happen in Thailand, too, as time would tell. It certainly came as no surprise to the Thai people who traveled in a culture where everything cost 125 percent of what it should.

In a limited way there was a bit of grim logic to some of this, seeing the little bribe here and there as a user tax of sorts, where the person getting the government service paid extra for it and the person not getting it paid no higher taxes to fund a decent salary for the official in the first place. But that implies a fairness of application, distribution or consequences which really seldom follows. Beyond any other merit, the man with the biggest bribe or kickback gets the contract, beyond justice the person with too little money alone feels the fist of the law or events while yet another can buy his way out of it. And public "servants" with tiny salaries can amass fortunes beyond the fantasies of business moguls, big bankers or baseball players.

Thailand may have been less corrupt than other places but corrupt it was indeed. Political power to appoint underlings to prosperous assignments came from bought-and-paid-for electoral victories. The money for the appointment came, ultimately, from the poor sap under the thumb of the appointed. Assignments went to cronies expected to

remember who did the assigning. Blinkers are expensive and the blink-
ered oversight authorities never quite managed to notice the siphoning
off of standards or money for contracts, for supplies, for service and
goods because they, in turn, so often had a tap into the siphon themselves. And it meant raw cash collected by the steamer trunk load. In
distant banks for safekeeping. Or hidden in safes in a closet. Or paying
for the lifestyles of the very wealthy indeed, being lead by agents and
officials not otherwise expected to travel in such pricey company. It
was big business.

The game was often so open that it was impossible not to notice.
Or not comment upon. Regularly, complaints went up from officials
maybe who were envious of the opportunities of a rival, for that rather
than from any strong sense of the injustice of it all to the people ultimately paying for it. Those at the top too often cared little for those
below except in assuring their cowed capacity to keep on paying. Accordingly, when the Bangkok World would write about corruption, we
were likely to hear the gnashing of very powerful teeth. We would see
the sparks when we wrote that the 40 million baht paid for a 20 million baht building was 30 million baht more than the thing was worth.
Or that so many of the millions authorized for aid to the poorer parts
of the country rather simply never got there.

We were appreciated when we wrote of the effects of a bad fire in a
poorer section of town, but got the cold glare when pointing out that
the fire engine ordered bought for such needs had never arrived since
the money to pay for it had vanished in the mist. Were the paper to
bemoan the effect of bribes and kickbacks, there were more murmured
oaths than over everything else we might do on the lofty matters of
public affairs or the complexity of the times. But write it we did. It
wasn't the only thing we wrote, but we wrote plenty about how corrupt
the political process so often was, how various factions rigged the rare

and already bogus elections, how public officials making a few hundred dollars a month lived like tycoons, how the public picked up the extra tab for a contract or a consideration bought and paid for by companies trying to do honest business – or what passed for such when the official hand was always out, when the bribes flowed like Singha beer on Patpong Road, when someone needed to pay for the approval to do a bit of necessary work. I'm not sure it did any good, and maybe the principal effect was making our own costs go up, making our staff's regular immigration challenges more costly and complex, but it needed to be said.

The pages of the daily paper would appear pretty conventional to Western readers: top local, national and international news in the front; sports inside, a section of business news, features and entertainment, social news; the editorial page; city news – which tended mostly to be stories about car and bus crashes (invariably, because if they couldn't catch you they couldn't punish you, ending with the signature line: "The driver fled the scene.") The Sunday magazine, when I first got there, was mostly snappy pictures of Thai life, animals at the zoo and interesting little features about local history or ancient events. Soon, we shifted that to more often include some of our most controversial and penetrating coverage of the great currents of the country and region. Taking advantage of the magazine's roomier space, there we ran deep examinations of the war, commentary on sweeping social developments, crisp reporting by Narong Ketudat on corruption and political hanky-panky and the weekly observations of our progressive economics columnist, GNP – a totally transparent cover for the irrepressible Mechai Viravaidya.

I usually blocked off a portion of Tuesday morning for the weekly harangue from the police or someone in the office of the mightily powerful Minister of the Interior field Marshal Praphas Charusathien, or some lesser general or minister. The paper's owners would get their own calls, too, which would be passed my way. I could set my watch by it: 8 a.m. morning news meeting; 8:45 advertising department session; 9:15 get yelled at and threatened by various ministers. Someone would point out the offending article to them on Monday and they'd spend the day gnawing on the table legs and working up a response and defense. On Tuesday they'd deliver the reaction, sometimes with the subtlety of a brick thrown through the window. Then it was all handshakes and "see you next week."

Mechai, a brilliant observer and penetrating analyst and thoughtful writer, would joke that the "GNP" stood not for anything from his beloved economics but, instead, for "persona non grata" in reverse. In reverse, too, – and exactly as it should be – it was me more often that got the "non grata" treatment for Mechai's "persona," the recurring excoriation of government decisions, misguided economic policies, social obtuseness and corruption. They seldom disputed his accuracy or even his judgment since he so clearly had the kingdom's very best interest deeply at heart; they just turned on the heat because someone had the audacity to say the truth in the first place. Or the second place.

It simply amazed and baffled them, his targets and critics, that we did this, notably when there was nothing particularly in it for us to be doing it. They could understand perfectly if a rival faction was huffing and puffing for its own piece of the pie, but we did it ... for nothing? These crazy farangs.

Narong's work, and that of his growing cadre of young, bright, idealistic reporters, focused on corruption and its effect on the nation's economy, image and soul. Narong, a son of privilege and authority himself, took it personally that corruption – economic and political – existed in such grim, debilitating excess. We published story after story about the vast wealth possible from gorging a huge construction project, say, or as important contract approvals passed through official hands. We diagrammed how much of the retail price of an item or the cost of a government service or a license to do routine business was puffed up by corrupt payments along the expensive line. I wish I could say that our efforts resulted in a cleansing of the system entirely – or even a bit – but there is no evidence whatever that it did. But we did our best, no matter how much the sparks might fly.

The Thai newspapers, maybe with a lot more at stake themselves, only lightly touched on such matters, choosing other battles to fight – unless a paper aligned with one faction was to air the depredations of some general or official from another faction. That was fair enough. And there were plenty to go around. The Bangkok Post did its part in such reporting as well, and likely the tiny English-language papers seemed to do more than the mighty local press combined. But staying in business was important to us all, and Thailand's various military governments had a long history of periodically cracking down on their opposition and critics. Some dancing is easily forgiven Thai journalists trying to keep their papers alive. They couldn't flee the scene.

The Thai government had any number of rules on the books that they could spring on an offending newspaper in the "national interest." Disrespect to the royal family, excessive bad taste, however it might be defined, a "bad reputation for accuracy"– whatever that might be pretzled to mean – could be adjudged and a paper and its officers endangered. Mostly, all the papers played close to the rules, even as we knew that the rules could mysteriously change, and often no one would know exactly what the new rules might be until someone found himself on the wrong side of them. Actually, the Thai sense of selectively respecting authority was such that there were few confrontations called for.

Once, though, the government let it be known that it was going to toughen up rules on the press, including opening the threat of pre-publication censorship "in the interests of national security," and the press sharply objected. As new regulations were being considered that the Thai press in particular objected to, many of the newspaper leaders met and it was determined that, to show the people the impact of censorship, no coverage would be delivered of the upcoming, January 1970, visit to Bangkok of the U.S. Vice President Spiro Agnew, himself ultimately exposed as such a total crook as to be almost a blood-brother of the corruption leaders elsewhere. No one invited the Bangkok World or the Post to weigh in on the decision for a total blackout, a decision with which I totally disagreed. The Bangkok Post went along with it, but we did run modest stories about Agnew's visit – but with me writing a front-page editorial describing how censorship was just as bad when done by ourselves as by the government, and possibly even more invidious; and we left the editorial page blank each day of the visit with a large black border, explaining that such could be the effect of government strangling a newspaper's soul.

Maybe it wasn't all that grand of a gesture but I just couldn't see the wisdom of self-suppression to protest suppression. To my surprise and huge relief, though, this was picked up by the Thai press, described as a bold move, all the more powerful because it was done in the wide open while the self-news-boycott of the other papers was invisible to those who did not know otherwise that Agnew was on the prowl at all. And when the Foreign Ministry reflexively sniffed that my dragging the contretemps out into the public was inconvenient for the Thai government's image and interests, that only made the Bangkok World look better to the news people whose backing I could need in a pinch. I modestly took the credit for bold wisdom while making no great show of the truth that, while very much meaning it, the protest was pretty much jerry-built. At the worst, once again, a few cranky critics knee-jerkingly allowed as you could hardly expect much better from the American-oriented newspaper, so clearly in the pocket of the CIA, etc., etc.

There were plenty of spook footprints – if a spook could leave footprints– in those days and pretty much everyone was rumored to be on someone's payroll, and whether it was true or not was seldom allowed to diminish the fun of creating rogues galleries of the town's MI-6, CIA, KGB, DCRI, etc., phantom pantheon. I'm not sure that any intelligence apparatus anywhere had a budget big enough to pay for all those imagined to be on it in Bangkok. With no evidence what-ever, everyone was held to be working for the CIA, for the British, for the Soviets, for the Japanese, for the various Chinese, for the Antarc-ticans. In the post-World War era, governments very likely did spread around the cash to back newspapers and other endeavors. The rumor was deep that the Bangkok World was flooded with CIA money. I almost wish it were so. If we had access to all the rumored cash, run-ning the paper might have been a lot easier. Maybe I would have even settled for access to American cigarettes, which cost what a bottle of good whiskey cost in those days. But no one offered us cigarettes. Or cash. And if they had, there'd be grounds aplenty for a malpractice lawsuit since my editorials and the paper's coverage was so relentlessly in the teeth of the very policies that those cigarettes would likely to have been given to support. But I never did see much evidence that the truth will very often deflect a good rumor, except over time, so I never lost a lot of energy trying to counter the claims of the shadowy and powerful forces believed to be behind us.

IN HIS ARCH WARNING, THANAT KHOMAN may have made an odd call on our lack of enthusiasm for R. M. Nixon of the 1600 block of Pennsylvania Avenue, as the District of Columbia police describe crime scenes, but Dr. Thanat was closer to right on the Burmese. Not "closer," he was *exactly* right. He had us on that.

Burma, or Myanmar as it is now known, was an unending challenge – principally to the poor Burmese, who suffered far more than any inconvenienced Thai diplomats under the hard heels of that military government's oppression. We had a large number of Burmese on the paper since there were a large number of Burmese refugees in Bangkok who had fled the oppression in the land next door and, because Burma had been a British colony, their English was so often excellent. Among them was Sterling Seagrave, a fifth-generation native of Asia and son of Dr. Gordon Seagrave, a world-famous physician, humanitarian and author who had run afoul of the Burmese authorities even before his son did. Sterling was married to Wendy Law-Yone, daughter of Edward Law-Yone, a crusading journalist, himself driven out of Burma by the Rangoon junta. Law-Yone's great courage and spirit animated his star-bright daughter, who went on to be a grand author.

Sterling was editor of the Sunday magazine, increasingly our showcase vehicle for deep issues, smart writing, snappy photography and controversy. There we created a forum for sharp opinion that didn't fit in the news pages, crisp essays and analysis from voices little heard elsewhere. Sterling did a great job, always, and pretty much followed the rules to stay away from things-Burma. Pretty much always. His was a strong voice in the miniature, collegial councils around office ashtrays that shaped the editorial content of the rest of the paper.

Enough so, apparently, that when I returned from a trip, I found that the paper had been running front pages stories describing the presumed fatal illness of the Burmese strongman, General Ne Win, and ultimately kissing off the blood-soaked tyrant as nearly dead and gone, at death's door and welcome it would be when he tumbled through it. The stories created a sensation. Except that, of course, General Ne Win was not dead and gone but quite alive and bad. The stories had come out of the totally unreliable, if hopeful, Burmese refugee crowd. The generals in Rangoon trotted out the usually camera-shy Ne Win as proof that the stories were so very wrong.

Running such badly sourced stories broke even the slipperiest rules of anyone's journalism. We were just wrong. After getting barked at by the Burmese ambassador for an hour, I called in Sterling and we agreed that he gone way too far, embarrassing the paper with what turned out to be wishful thinking and which undercut our vital need for professionalism and reliability. We shook hands on it, agreeing that it was time for him to go. Goodbye, Sterling.

Except that on the way out the door he sneaked into a silly magazine feature we ran – bogus captions applied to actual news or feature photos – the photo of the Burmese dictator shaking hands with someone but with a cartoon balloon over Ne Win's head saying, "Well, you'll have to excuse me now but I have to climb back into my iron lung."

More barking.

Not that there's any excuse whatever for being so wrong, notably when there's likely to be a personal motive behind being so wrong, but it's hard enough to work up too much sympathy for the supposedly delicate diplomatic feelings of the Burmese military government thuggery, which would go on for long and painful decades. But wrong we were. We didn't set out to make things more difficult for the Thai authorities when it came to dealings with the other, much-meaner military junta across the border, but more difficult it was – and more so later when I wandered into yet another tricky bit of Thai-Burmese sensitivity.

A year or so later, and although now I can barely imagine why, I considered it a good idea to go a-wandering in the tough mountainous jungles along the invisible border in northwest Thailand in pursuit of an interview with the head of the Karen National Liberation Army which, then and nearly forever after, was fighting the Burmese government in what became one of the world's longest civil wars. The Burmese tended to kick the stuffing out of the Karen peoples, one of the largest tribes in the richly diverse and complex nation, and many took to the jungles to fight the oppressive junta. Identifying forces fighting against the government in Rangoon, as it was then called, was not difficult; finding them was a bit harder. Prasong Wittaya, the Bangkok World's senior Thai editor, a Reuters reporter friend and I got it into our heads to drop in for tea at a jungle encampment of Karen fighters that we'd gotten wind of, a bit of adventure that seemed important at the time – risking our dumb necks jungle-trekking for a story that hopefully some six people would possibly care about beyond Burma – but one maybe casting some light on the brave Karen struggle.

Of course the whole point of rebel jungle encampments is to be hard to get to, since dodging the authorities is entirely part of the job description of being a rebel in the first place. For days we scratched our way – by jeep, by foot, even on elephant back! – through the gloriously beautiful landscape populated only by squawky birds, postage stamp colored butterflies the size of a Christmas card, mosquitoes like pub darts, some creepy snakes and huge ugly spiders looking like windblown toupees. There were scattered hill tribes and a few traders suspiciously more likely to be agents of the heroin-moving drug lords than anyone interested in conducting high commerce in the airy jungle wilds.

At night, it was all spooky noises and strange rustlings as creatures prowled their territory so rudely intruded upon by the visitors from the city. By day the vision was mostly of the sides of trees under the canopied cover, which would burst free and open at some curve to reveal beautiful valleys, lined by craggy rock peaks, created by the deep-slicing Salween River below. It was very hot. There were bugs there the size of small birds, and I was far more afraid of them than I was of any government or rebel soldiers.

We'd happen onto small villages, just clusters of thatch-covered houses on stilts, and the people would come out to greet us, and then nearly recoil in anxious amazement at the pink creature with the wild blue eyes and thatch-covered head. That would be Me. They would stare at me as if I had several extra noggins, and the children would inch forward to touch my arm as if I were some sort of wild creature from the deepest scary jungles. As I was, I suppose. In my early days in Korat, the waitresses at the camp officers' club – a mercilessly merry bunch – would giggle at my pathetic paleness, and I had the nickname among them along the line of "kwai chom poo," which was what they called the pink albino water buffalo occasionally in a farmers' otherwise black and grey herds. I'm sure they pronounced their tones right so that the handle wasn't even more of an eyebrow-raiser than it already was. I appreciated that to be called a water buffalo is not always the highest compliment among the Thais and that to be compared to a buffalo is no compliment either to me or the buffalo, but these laughing beauties did it with such happy mischief that who could complain? They did have the truth to fall back on, after all. Among the hill villagers, though, the fascination, if that's what it was, was that they rather simply had never seen such a thing before. I was more likely considered a defect rather than some visiting deity to whom they should present gold and baskets of fruit. They did offer fruit, however.

We reached the camp of Karen rebel leader Ma Zha Ban and his hundreds of well-armed, well-provisioned fighters in an orderly field of tents and huts near the edge of the Salween, a mighty river that hurls itself with great force down from the base of the distant Himalayas, cutting through the rocky hills with great power and which, at this point, marked the border between Burma and Thailand. This is no languid Chao Phrya or log-raft gliding Mississippi but a foamy, surging, white-water demon, which, among the trees and hills created a sight of nature's amazing authority. We talked with Ma Zha Ban for a while about his goals to fight for a separate status for his people, free of the Rangoon government's outrages. He vowed to battle on, sought the understanding and support of others who might sympathize with his peoples' plight. We shared a meal, rice and beans, I think, which had monkey and leopard in it. And we started home to Bangkok, following our trail backwards, back through those villages where the kids were now slightly less amazed at the arrival of the pinkster, across the ankle-chilling streams, again often atop the little elephant that carried the supplies, over the ridges – and into trouble.

I didn't know, but should have anticipated, that the travels of such obvious outsiders through the wildernesses was closely watched by Thai officials, and that the word had gone back to the capital while we were lumbering around with the big spiders. The Thai government was very sensitive to being called out for any support – actual or winking – for rebel forces fighting to overthrow the Burmese junta, or to wring a few concessions for the Karens, Shans and other victims of the harsh hand of Rangoon. The Thais had little affection for the Burmese generals but neither was there any interest in adding to the tensions and problems already accumulating on the Thai plate. Unknown to me, a police general had called on Dr. Chaijudh Karnasuta, the esteemed Thai partner of the Ital-Thai Corporation, advising him that his little newspaper should not be making problems where there was no need for new problems, thank you very much. Dr. Chaijudh, a fine man, wise and patient and caring, agreed. He planned to talk to me when I returned.

Dr. Chaijudh was a man of great presence and I had great respect for him. I would never have done anything to make life difficult for him if I could help it. The "if I could help it" proved to be the difficult part.

Coming back to the city, my insides were a-boil and a-bubble with the reaction my innards regularly produced after eating such things as monkey and leopard and drinking water in the wilds, either of the jungles or of Bangkok itself. Travel writers and other such shamsters are always waxing exuberant over the delicacies to be gobbled up from streetside vendor carts and plucked from wilderness vines; good for them, but such foods pretty much always made me sick. I suffered case after case of dysentery just from eating unwisely in the city. A stroll through the wilds left me even worse off. Weary and sick, I had written my story along the way back and I arrived quietly at the paper, had a few photos developed and arranged to have the story put in the next day's edition. I stumbled home without learning at all that Dr. Chaijudh had some advice for me concerning my sojourn in the jungles.

Fortunately, I did appreciate some of the international complexities of the situation. Beyond having no desire whatever to tip off the Burmese junta to the locale of the rebel camp, I understood that if I wrote that the camp was on the Burma side of the river, I could get in real trouble for having gone to Burma without anyone's legal permission. If I wrote that the camp was in Thailand, the Burmese would merrily thump the Thais over the head for that – and the thump would dutifully be passed along to me. Therefore, I wrote as my dateline for the interview: "Midstream in the Salween River." It was as if we were chatting in duck-headed rubber tubes such as they have in swimming pools, astraddle the border. Of course the Salween has no midstream, unless you count the froth and blasting careen of water smashing past in mad stampede; I might as well have written "Halfway Down Niagara Falls."

There was more barking from the Burmese, of course, but it was sort of out of focus since they couldn't deny that the Karens were out there. The Thai government officials gave me a case of the frigids for a while, but I hadn't caused them the huge problem that could have arisen from any suggestion that the Karens were camping on Thai soil. Dr. Chaijudh rubbed his kind, generous forehead and probably wondered who on earth thought that having a newspaper in the portfolio or having such as me running it would be a bright idea. He was a good man and was far too much of a gentleman to make the point that, well, maybe he deserved more peace of mind than that.

INTREPID JUNGLE-WANDERING wasn't dominant in the job description but it was part of the newspapering adventure, an experience little likely to be open to me had I gone on to work in a bank or, more likely, a shoe shop. Over my career I have worked for some four decades at the newspaper business and don't know that I ever had a boring day. It wasn't necessarily spiders in the jungles or frisky circuses in Moscow, but it was always interesting. For me and everyone else down with the wonderful newspapering malady.

Bangkok in those days was a rich and vibrant hubbub of journalists passing through, and some few using it as a base of operations to cover the wars nearby. The weekly luncheons of the Foreign Correspondents Club at the Oriental Hotel were always fascinating, a clearinghouse of news, gossip and hijinks among the press who rattled around the combat, so often risking their very lives and limbs for one more paragraph or a photo caption. Every major story brings out its own texture of news coverage and the Vietnam War crew was a hardy, spicy, profane and brilliant bunch. And needed to be.

In that age before satellite links and laptops that would work on the backside of Mr. Armstrong's moon or deep in the most tangled jungles, the technology of newsgathering was much the same as in Herodotus' day: See it. Think about it. Write it. Sometimes the dispatches would be written on notebook pages and hand-carried out of the country. Commercial pilots and flight attendants in Saigon could be often counted upon to ferry out film and more, where runners would meet them at Don Muang and other airports to process and forward the materials to the world. The reporters, photographers and technicians would often come to Bangkok for respite, for their own diversions.

I got to know many of them well as we would share experiences and observations and where I would help many with dealings in Thailand. To a one, they brought back the same truth – that the war in Indochina was failing even if there were those who simply refused to accept that, there or far away back home. A good friend, who was a key Time magazine correspondent covering the war, would come back with the most dire tales of the ineptitude of the South Vietnamese government and military; he filed story after story about the grim turning of events there and how very badly things were unfolding. Yet Time would then run story after story about how wonderfully the war was going, how noble and accomplished were the Vietnamese generals and leaders. I'd say to my friend, "What's going on here?" and he'd say, "Well, they have their own view on the war." After watching him put himself in such danger for an employer who would rewrite his accurate reporting I'd ask, "How can you continue to work for them?" "But it's *Time*," he'd say. "How can you not work for Time?"

A variety of German magazines enlisted the freelance service in Bangkok of Gustav Dietrich, who was a lively friend. Smart. Fun. Wizened. Once Gustav had been commissioned by one of the magazines to take lots of pictures of hottie-tottie Thai bar-babes and prostitutes. Being a hard-working sort, this was an assignment he carried out with gusto. They never said why they wanted the pictures, but a job was a job. He had pretty much forgotten the assignment until he was called into the Thai foreign ministry months later where they asked him about the complexities of the German language. "What exactly does 'schwesteren' mean?" he was asked. "Why, it means 'sisters,' " he replied – upon which time he was yelled at and threatened for hours as a copy of the magazine was rubbed into his face with its mean headline "Schwesteren der Sirikit" insultingly associating the pictures of the bar girls with the most beloved and beautiful Queen Sirikit. You could go to jail for such as that and a Thai jail would not at all be a pleasant place to be when the word got out behind the bars that you were there for so deeply insulting the Queen. Gustav was lucky to be able to successfully plead his innocence, to swear his vast love for the Queen and the country and his Thai wife as evidence that no one in his right mind would link her majesty the Queen to the sleazy Patpong Road scene. On the sly, he continued to provide copy and pictures for the magazine; he couldn't afford to lose the client.

Not that I didn't already have plenty to do, but I agreed to write pieces for the Far Eastern Economic Review, a respected, left-oriented magazine put out in Hong Kong and distributed widely around Asia. On a trip I had met and very much liked the Review's feisty editor, Derek Davies, and we traveled around together across the Pacific and the United States as I was heading home for a visit and he was traveling back to England on a holiday. I watched, or listened, with amusement as Derek's accent thickened or ebbed in different locales and relaxed as he got closer to the Greenwich Meridian –an effect, or affect, of expatriatism: John Gielgud on the road, Benny Hill at home. He asked me to write for the Review and I thought that was not a bad idea. I think they paid about $10 an article and I don't remember ever getting the money. But never mind, I liked the association.

I did the odd piece on politics and the Thai view of the war for the Review but probably underreported on the economy, which I hardly understood, despite it being so vital to a journal with "Economic" in the title. I walked away from the association when the magazine started taking sly potshots at the Thai king for no real reason; even without Gustav Dietrich's experience or that of the man from Time, I knew when there wasn't much to be gained for me in the link. In that, I got out one step ahead of the sheriff as the Thai government later unleashed a firestorm on the Far Eastern Economic Review, banning it for a time. It was all great sport to Derek, whose magazine was variously banned off and on everywhere in autocratic Asia but, with my own knack for getting into hot water, I'd figured I'd rather choose my own fights.

The press corps of the Vietnam War years was a terrific bunch – so often brave, honest, hard-working. They went into war zones with and without permission and came back with stories that spoke truth about an enterprise where truth was not always valued at all. There were those in the military and official American corridors who considered the reporters to be nearly as much the enemy as the black pajama'd Viet Cong and green uniformed North Vietnamese regulars who, by then, were doing so much of the fighting across Laos, Vietnam and Cambodia. The U.S. military so wrongheadedly tried to discredit and undermine the news people, as if the telling of the facts was somehow not in the national interest, as if the parents of soldiers, the citizenry and decision-makers, needed to be spared from reporting that demonstrated pretty conclusively that American war policies were not working and that thousands and thousands of people were dying as a result. The truth did eventually come out, of course, though much too late for those who had died and suffered so much in consequence.

I LIKE TO THINK THAT I WAS well thought-of by the Bangkok World staff. That would be nice. The staff was so much a hard-working, talented, energetic bunch and it took me a lot of work and compromise and dancing to protect their jobs as the economic noose tightened around the paper over time. Well-liked, though? I'd have no way of knowing. Sure, the Australians or Dutch aboard might well suggest openly that I was a 24-karat dope and the Brits or French might look wryly askance at my every brainstorm. But the Thais always told me that I was the wisest man in the entire universe, a paradigm of journalistic standard and acumen, a wizard of near demigod status. Me? Now, it is not at all that the Thai have very strange standards indeed but, rather, that they are very, very polite people indeed who would rather discomfort themselves than tell too much of the truth if it were to discomfort someone else.

To a fair degree, there was high pantomime, or something as amazingly stylized as the Ram Muay of Thai boxing, in the relationship between much of the Thai staff and the farangs, the foreigners, who cluttered up the easiness of their work lives. Intelligent and usually amiable folk, they did not want to displease, sometimes to the point of not ever delivering a straight answer if the answer was feared to be unsettling, even when the straightness of the answer's knowledge would be helpful and necessary. If I asked someone to check how we were doing in the scratchy matter of this official or that, I would always hear that everything was just fine, that there was nothing but the most grand affection towards the paper and especially its brilliant leadership under that Horgan chap who was so dazzling and so ... only to learn later that the officials were kicking the trash baskets around in rage at something we had done. If I needed to know, even, when a shipment of paper or supplies was to arrive it was always "any minute," "any second," even when the messenger had learned that the materials were long delayed and that there would be costly consequences. I learned that you had to ask the same question four times and study the slight differences in the answers, to conjure up from the shadows and the pauses between the words and the variations of expression, for some hopeful understanding of what the truth might be. They didn't want anyone to be displeased.

Usually.

One day, I arrived back in the office to find the place in turmoil, more even than usual. A violent argument – violent on one side, anyway – had broken out in which a stormy European copy editor had ferociously menaced another, the latter being the very honored and true gentleman Mr. Das Gupta, widely respected and beloved by all, quite in contrast to the fiery European. It was apparently a terrible scene, with the whole place rich with anger and outrage and the furniture fairly trembled with the vibration still later when I got back after lunch. Even before I got to sit down, Mr. Gupta came to my little office and said that it was all a misunderstanding, most unfortunate, but that there was no need for it to go any further. That would be Mr. Gupta. He had barely left when in stormed a member of the composing room staff, raging and being restrained by several others, who argued tearfully and, I fear, drunkenly, that this was a huge insult to Mr. Gupta and the ordering of the planets and that the European should be made to pay dearly, and on and on like that until he was hauled away still shouting by his friends and colleagues. Back came Mr. Gupta to entreat that the whole thing was already far too distressing and that it, please, should all be forgotten. This was flowing around so quickly that I don't imagine that I was able to have said two words, but I hoped that, indeed, it would all be set aside. It nearly was.

As far as I knew Mr. Gupta and the other man never had another problem; but that evening the drunken fellow from the back shop returned after I had left and, drunker still, pulled out a pistol and, apparently enraged that I had failed to deliver justice to the offending European, proceeded to shoot my chair, my empty chair fortunately. Away he was hauled yet again, the planet's sense of honor eased while only my poor chair was the one which got plugged. I kept that bullet for a while but lost it over time.

I have known since uncountable editors and executives who probably deserve to have been shot at by the staff but count it a distinct if unusual honor to be the only one to whom the practice has been even symbolically applied.

THE DISTINCTIONS OF AUTHORITY are crisply defined in the Thai workplace and society, a land where strata of rank are drawn and respected with exquisite care. The fertile nobility has been around for so long that they needed to dismember the class structure a little lest the land overflow with princes and their princelings. In the more familiar to me British or European aristocracy I have never quite understood when a duke outranks a count or whether a marquise can boss around a baron; but I do know there are far too many of them. There was some cautious sense of that in Thailand, too. In fact, the children of princes are automatically calibrated down to the title of mom rajawongse and their descendants are knocked off a further notch, designated mom luang, while *their* children are without any such rank at all, skinnying up the supply of rank over a few generations – even as new ones might be added at the top. Military levels in a military government abounded. The prime minister then was a field marshal. The minister of the interior was also a field marshal. field marshals, if you will. This from a military that, excepting a few, had hardly ever fought anyone at all yet one where the tiptop carried the ranks of a Wellington or Zhukov, a Montgomery or Foch. field marshal, my foot. The Thai military still has two times as many active duty general officers than does the distinctly larger and markedly better American force. There is power in rank. Wealth, and there was a great deal of it in commercial and other hands, had its own power, too, of course, and the giants of commerce and banking lived like near-royalty themselves. Maybe more so. But the poorest mom luang commanded a sway from his bloodline to rank with the wealthiest business tycoon or mightiest beribboned general.

Lacking title or fortune, advancement for the rest was cautiously possible by the familiar paths of accomplishment: skill and education. As the society shrugged itself awake from centuries of soft isolation and comfortable inaction, the economy began to boom; international and business opportunities needed more bright people than could ever be supplied by the ranks of royalty or wealth alone. Education was wisely seen as the key to all success, and educators since even before the days of King Mongkut were granted honored status across the land. To be a teacher – an archarn – is a revered distinction, even as teachers there as everywhere are still poorly paid. You can never quite calculate where the cynicism begins and ends but probably it's wise to put your hand over your wallet when people are singing your vital job's noble praises for it so often happens that when they ratchet up the respect they discount down the salary. In Thailand, though, to be a teacher was certainly to an honored position, whatever the pay packet. Thailand has an important national teachers day, and takes it very seriously. Likely, too, such praise can go to your head.

Midstream in my time at the Bangkok World the owners hired a new general manager, after some concern of rascality and suspected skimming off of tidy amounts of money from short-weighed, thumb-on-the-scale newsprint shipments. The new general manager was

Archarn Phayung, a young former university teacher – once a teacher, always a teacher – who had married into the owner's family. He was honest. He was clear-eyed. He moved with the authority of a school master, and was granted such respect almost always. He did come up short on the rascality quotient and was annoyingly rules oriented but he was a good man otherwise, accustomed to being heeded. His title of general manager was important, but everyone still called him "archarn."

After midnight one morning, Phayung knocked on our door to say that the circulation crew had refused to deliver the papers to our subscribers, demanding huge increases in their pay or they would keep us from getting the Bangkok World to the readers. Strikes were illegal in Thailand but they seemed not to care. Phayung, in full archarn-mode, was outraged at the affront and had found out where the group was gathering, so off we went in his car to get them back to work. We discovered the twenty or so young men and their motorcycles on the expansive marble parade grounds outside the gigantic Parliament building which glowed beautifully in the street lights and brilliant moon above. There they were, huffing and puffing in their nervous energy, and largely drunk. Phayung drove his car right up to the group, immediately popped out and began assailing the men as if they were school children, commanding them to obey his orders, to do what they were told, to ...

Before I could get around the car from my side, the drunken crew had grabbed lofty Archarn Phayung and were tossing him around like a doll, slipping in punches and thumps in the process. I jumped in to try to rescue the poor man and some of the crowd, of course, turned on me. It happened all in a flash, shouts ringing and re-echoing off the marble, and then it all seemed to fall into the most amazing slow motion and dead silence as I pushed off this guy and that one only to see the crowd open up and two red-eyed, reeling men come at me – one with a knife and the other with a piece of jagged wood. As they lunged at me together, they just missed on either side, the knife passing under one of my arms, the sharp wooden sword-point under the other. Instinctively my hands somehow went out and caught their two heads just before me, and I rammed them together with a terrible cracking sound that reverberated like a cannon shot off the marble all around. The men fell to the ground in a heap. "Oh, man, I've killed them both," I thought. Instead, after an excruciating silence when everything else froze, the two men soon slowly got to their hands and knees, then to their feet, stumblingly offered me a clumsy, pained *wai* – hand's together in respect salute – and were carried away by the now-very-sober crowd. They went back to work: This had gone far, far beyond anyone's expectation. Theirs. Phayung's. Mine.

I got into Phayung's car, trembling at the unintended violence and wild emotion of the moment. Phayung was even more shocked. "Do you believe what just happened! I am a teacher," he said dizzyingly. "I am the archarn. Did you see how they treated me?" I was too jingle-jangle to offer, "Archarn, my ass, pal. They tried to *kill me*." It was his judgment that the greater disrespect had been visited upon him. Fair enough. Editors come and go, I guess. Archarns are immortal.

Business 'As Usual'

FOR ALL THE NIFTY TRAVEL and the diplomatic hobnob, the forays into odd places, the parties, the true essence of the Bangkok World experience was the hard work and professionalism required by one and all to get it through the day; ultimately, its gravest challenges came not from any cranky government ministry or painters of naked ladies but from old fashioned business problems.

The economics of producing an English-language newspaper vary with the ZIP code but invariably they are daunting. The Bangkok World's circulation was in the area of 13,000 a day and there was simply no prospect of advancing that number much higher. There were only so many English-speakers around and available. The Bangkok Post chimed it at more than 15,000 and we could imagine that between us, separately and overlapping, we already had just about everyone we could get. If there were another dozen readers hidden away in distant Chiang Rai or Yala provinces it wouldn't make any financial sense to go after them. Even someone so untrained in matters commercial as I could see that. Clearly then, success depended on finding a level of cost and revenue that would hit the right sustainable balance.

We very well might have had a few too many people on board but, frankly, the Bangkok World paid folks so little that it hardly seemed to make any difference. Working long hours I figured I would never see my wife, Pat, otherwise, so I hired her as an editor – and would have snapped my fingers under the nose of any anti-nepotism-fetishists who so object to practices like that. Give me western protections and traditions and I'll consider western rules. Besides, she was paid even less than the going rate of some $200 a month of other copy editors. My own astronomical salary just barely hit five figures a year. As it was, with hard work at cutting costs, our slim operating revenues actually, if slightly, exceeded our operating expenses in the early days. The mysteries of capital needs and other murky financial matters were handled elsewhere and it was my job to work with what I could.

I calculated that if we cut services and staff too much, a largely discretionary product would become ever-less desirable for its busy readers. There was no particular retail advertising to expand as most department stores and markets knew there weren't enough foreign customers to shop there much – so it was the movies and travel world and entertainment that best supported us. Attracting more readers among the U.S. servicemen was of little help for, beyond any pride and vanity we might have in a bigger number, the advertisers didn't care that more people on distant isolated military bases were reading our paper as they weren't likely to be buying the advertised products. In fact, the more we sold up-country the more it cost us in newsprint and shipping. Maybe I should have let them throw the papers off the train after all.

The many airlines doing business in Thailand would agree to a fixed amount of advertising for which they would pay in cash, but they usually seemed ready to expand on the pages if we would accept tickets instead of money. This barter system worked well for us – and allowed us to send staff members on the most amazing adventures, rewarding good service and getting good coverage, better than might be possibly imagined otherwise. Importantly, we used most of the tickets at the parent company, Ital-Thai, which worked well on the accounting side, getting credit for their travel at no great cash cost at either end.

For the paper's use, I actually kept in a little tin box vouchers for airline tickets, and I would dole out ducats to London or the Riviera to worthy staffers the way that Rockefeller of old would hand his thin dimes to the hoi polloi. Pat and I covered the wedding of the Crown Prince of Nepal on such tickets, racking up grand stories and experiences for the out-of-pocket price of a weekend in a hotel. (In those times aircraft landed on the little strip in the Vale of Kathmandu pretty much the way a small log landed after being dropped from hawk's feet. The plane needed to circle around the steep-walled, deep valley to lose speed before arcing in for a landing, giving the folks on the earthward side a straight-down view out the window of the beautifully terraced rice paddies cut over the centuries into the hillsides. The plane careened to the runway and all-but threw out an anchor to stop in time. The Pakistani ambassador told us of his particularly rough slam to the ground: "From every mouth came a shout!") The paper covered a world cricket championship in India, flying for free. If there was a significant ASEAN conference in Manila, we sent a staffer on barter tickets since there was no chance we'd be there otherwise. I had my serious professional standards but I never exactly tried to superimpose too many distinctly American practices on a distinctly non-American world of Thai newspapering. Certainly there was no first Amendment to keep me from starting a bit at a knock at the door after dark or the squint of the military government's archly sensitive agents. So, fair and square, we bartered space for tickets.

But you can't eat airplane tickets.

With expenses pretty much fixed and traditional revenues largely locked in, I felt that we needed to develop new money streams and new products. This was a view also followed by the Bangkok Post which launched an afternoon edition, and we quickly had to match unless we were to be left behind. The Bangkok World already had a Sunday magazine and I soon added a series of other daily products to lure in new revenue. On Mondays we printed The New York Times' Week in Review section, minus the editorial pages. This was considered an amazing technological accomplishment around town when, in fact, we merely had them air freight out to us crisp photo-ready page proofs which we copied and ran with our own name in the margins. Slap on a page or two of ads and it made money. On Tuesdays we started a Punch Magazine section, a pure cut-and-paste operation from proofs of that humor magazine also shipped to us by air. There was no need for extra staff to get these out, only extra newsprint. For Wednesdays, we produced and distributed an ad-free student edition, put together to teach the basics of English and math and the like for children. This we sold to the Bangkok school system, moving more than 30,000 copies a week to schools in the city. Because the law forbade newspapers to print separate elements without a license, we designated the section as an extension to the daily paper and included it to our readers only with the Bangkok editions. As much as I might be confident that such basic training might well do some good among my old pals in the up-country military, we spared them the effort of discarding it unread. On Fridays we clumped together entertainment copy and nightlife pictures into a weekend edition. These supplements brought in a little more money – the Punch section, for example, appealing to the British advertisers who by preference, custom or direction otherwise advertised only with the British-owned Bangkok Post.

More, we expanded the special editions to mark national days, special holidays and King Bhumipol's birthday and that of Queen Sirikit. Who could decline to advertise in a section honoring the royal family?

Wringing endorsements from the various embassies, we shook down every company and community with the vaguest link to, say, France or Bolivia, and came up with a special advertisement section hailing the policies, leaders and people of those lands as the most brilliant anywhere on the planet. With ample warning as to the commercial nature of the project, we would write up scruffy national brigands as if they were Gandhi, King Arthur of Camelot and Honest Abe Lincoln combined, every economy was a stellar success, every social and cultural swamp became Manhattan and Soho and the Louvre rolled together. You'd be surprised at how many countries could be so exuberantly praised, surely making our Martian subscribers consider the earth as a paradise indeed in the otherwise drab cosmos.

THE BANGKOK WORLD'S PROSPECTS were shaky, yes, but no one could blame Trink.

Possibly there was a U.S. soldier somewhere in the crusty corners of the northeast, or an airman tightening bolts on the Wild Weasels and B52s, who read the Bangkok World for its penetrating political analysis of Southeast Asian affairs or the economic vagaries reflected on the business pages. Maybe. I never met him, though. More likely the hard working eye or libidinous gaze of the military guy turned first to the odd work of Bernard Trink, the World's "Nite Owl."

Trink – and he was never, "Bernie" or "Bernard" – had drifted into Thailand a few years earlier from Japan where he had done pick-up work writing movie reviews and such for papers there. In Thailand he found a match that was made in some Trink Heaven. And at the Bangkok World he found his pulpit – although to compare things religious with things Trink is to invite eternal hellfire in the toasty hereafter.

Trink brought his tin cinematic ear to movie reviews, yes, but it was working the bars and strip clubs of Bangkok's energetic, bawdy

Patpong Road and other salons of the salacious for which the town is so noted that he has made his curious mark – and sold us a lot of newspapers.

Working like a demon in his signature white short-sleeve shirt, short black tie and trousers belted up just under his nipples, Trink certainly never missed a new movie in the city's modest foreign cinema scene. Only rarely did he review the Thai movie scene and, in fact, one review a year would have done it as the Thai movies of those days were pretty much all the same: beautiful innocent country girl falls in love; she loses boyfriend to the glitzy uber-world of the Big City or to the wiles of a conniving rich lady; all seems lost for her; but, hooray, boy and girl are reunited amid a monsoon of tears and bright lights and song. I sort of liked Thai movies, as even I could figure out what was going on, and the actors were all handsome and beautiful and, since they allowed you to eat and drink in your seat in Thai theaters, it was all a picnic anyway.

But it was Trink's Nite Owl ramblings that were to so many gnarled ids the somewhat cheesy landmark of the paper and its town. Each Friday he would have page after page of accounts of the saucy mayhem in the boozeries so popular with tourists, soldiers, expatriates and Thais, too. He kept everyone aware of who was singing, what new chanteuses and danseurs were in from the boonies to wriggle and warble with diminishing clothes as the songs progressed. He catalogued the new bar girls on assignment, noting that Miss Lek had moved from the Purple Parrot to the Happy Home, that Miss Ratana had developed quite an imaginative naked acrobatics at the Palm Door and which of the chanteuses at Club Gow-Sip-Gow were also entertaining on a smaller stage afterwards. And there were pictures. Risking the virtue of our poor photographers and sometimes taking his own misty snapshots, there would be shot after shot of the lovely young women in the postage-stamp-sized costumes of the steamy night.

And, because he was Trink, hundreds of those pictures ended up stuck on the walls around his desk, the cubicle right outside my own office door. The pictures, many with the grease pencil croppings still on them, were glued and pinned to the partitions and rose up the wall beyond head high. Not exactly the Sistine Chapel, but nearly as distinctive.

One day we were dedicating a new press building and Prime Minister Thanom Kittikachorn was due to come by and ceremoniously press the button that would start the presses following the monks' blessing and before the champagne's popping. The simple plan had field Marshal Thanom to stroll through the newsroom en route to the pressroom ceremony, so I said to Trink, "Those pictures have to come down." He moaned and railed away in protest but I was firm: It's the prime minister, for cryeye. No pictures of naked bar girls. Take them down.

Well, with climate-changing sighs, he did it. Not a picture of the hundreds of his tawdry Lascaux cave was to be seen. The Prime Minister strolled through the room, pushed his button and was gone, all in about five minutes. We returned to the newsroom in satisfaction and discovered that all the pictures, each and every one of them, were back up again exactly as before! It was a miracle. A Trink miracle.

Trink was a loner who never actually bought into the idea that he worked for anyone else. You could order him to do something, and several times out of twenty he would actually follow the command. But he would barely think to alert you that your necktie was dipping into the soup at lunch.

He had married a Thai woman and, to prove how strong are the Thai beauty chromosomes, they had a lovely little son, a bright-eyed little dazzler, all smiles and grins. One day I was fiddling around in my office with a new camera and the little boy, about three years old, wandered into the room in the way little boys will and rummaged around and brightened up the place enormously. I took a few pictures of him and, as he was so beautiful, they came out very well. I had a few prints made and left them on Trink's desk. Soon he came into my office, the pictures in his almost-trembling hands. He asked if these were from me; I said they were. He nodded and went out and was back in a minute or so and placed wordlessly on my desk several Scandinavian pornographic magazines. He backed out the door without saying anything. It was touching in its odd Trink way. He was repaying my gesture in his own currency.

As the years went along and as the fortunes of the English-language papers in Bangkok shifted and swerved, Trink almost alone survived one era after another. Good for him. He earned it, in his unique way.

USING EXISTING STAFF, we were batting out a madhouse of newspapering. Two editions a day. Magazines. Special supplements. Holiday packages. And the other guys were doing a lot of the same thing, too. Readers in Thailand had every right to be amazed at what they got for their paltry nickels. Huge papers in the United States then and now did and do less.

It could hardly be expected to go on forever.

When I was hired, the Bangkok World was very largely owned by the Ital-Thai empire, with a tiny sliver in the hands of an American lawyer and stockbroker, a token Yank. In so many ways, the owners knew the local scene, its vagaries and strengths, its pulsing growth and political tremors. They were engaged in the economic structure of the kingdom, prospered with its prosperity, understood the significance of changes in the political and cultural winds. Owning a newspaper produced the possibility of a voice in the nation's increasingly complex debates. Or maybe a shield – if sometimes, too, a target. To my sure knowledge, the Bangkok World's owners never abused it. They never asked for special treatment, for us to change the shape of the coverage, to favor a friend or belittle a foe. It was comforting to have them behind us when the inevitable bickering with the government might erupt. Whatever little the paper might cost them to run in the huge scheme of their things, they seemed ready to endure. So I thought.

But one day early in the spring of 1970 they called me in and announced that they had just sold a large interest in the enterprise to a collection of American fatcats and this would surely give us the resources to grow and provide stability to prosper forevermore. And these cats were fat indeed. Headed up by James Linen III, bossissimo of the gargantuan Time Inc. empire, and his son, James Linen IV, who ran a string of newspapers in Illinois, the group included such heavyweights as the heads of American Express, Seagrams, and the like. Wow, I thought.

Wow, indeed. Put together at the suggestion of the meddling State Department which had an eye to waving the red, white and blue most vigorously over a Bangkok newspaper, the Linen Group, as it was always called, was made up of 24-karat bigtimers who bought in for the price of new presses and printing equipment. We would get modern electronic typesetting gear, the supporting plate-making apparatus and a big photo-offset press capable of zipping out tidy numbers of papers as never before. No one asked me whether I thought there was a market enough to sustain such razzle-dazzle toys, but I could only assume that these mighties knew what they were doing, as successful as they were in everything else they did. They knew enough to send out one of their number, the estimable John A. Millington from Time, Inc., to represent their interests and guide the enterprise's commercial affairs as managing director. That was a terrific development all in itself. A great spirit, wondrously intelligent and deft, John ran the business side of the paper with flair and imagination before personal and family matters resulted in him going back to the United States, a very sad loss for us personally and to the Bangkok World itself.

Dropping new presses and typesetting equipment into developing Bangkok was no easy thing; the system took an enormous amount of work to set up – so much so that the staff toiled around the clock, some of us even sleeping on John Millington's office floor for a few hours some nights in total exhaustion – including Pat who was very pregnant indeed with the upcoming little storm cloud over Bangkok. By enormous work and energy, the staff finally muscled the thing to work but we quickly discovered that the cost of running the new process was so much more than anyone planned or even wildly anticipated.

The concept of the white elephant gift was born precisely in Southeast Asia, where, in fact, an elephant rarely does indeed qualify as being white. Not chalky white in the way a polar bear is white or as is a swan or Moby Dick, but a bit paler-than-usual elephant with fair eyelashes and special toenails. To possess a white elephant is seen as a sign of sacred power, great good fortune, that a monarch was wise, reigning in peace with justice and prosperity. But there is more than mere legend to the idea that to give someone a white elephant is to put the poor fool on the road to ruination. The white elephant is expected to be maintained in its own palace and with a lifestyle as is enjoyed by mere human potentates and tycoons. An elephant is an elephant, but the upkeep will be the end of you. The modern equivalent is the uncle's sly holiday gifts to the annoying nephews which require fifteen batteries which last, each, for ten minutes. So it is that the concept of something being a "white elephant" is no gift or compliment at all.

The new printing system was beautiful to see finally in operation

– once we flew in the extra typesetting units that it proved we needed – but it required enormously expensive upkeep, costly imported supplies and constant maintenance often from technicians not at all available to be found in Bangkok, Thailand. Until then, paying the paltry wages of two dozen or more typesetters was bearable since the paper actually played slightly ahead on operating expenses over revenues. The future surely would be bright. Somehow. We retrained and kept as many of the old hands as we could. It was hoped that the new look of the paper and its modern, future-leaning approach would attract more readers and advertisers and pay for itself and more. Maybe in time that would have happened. Turns out, we didn't have the time.

It wasn't only the new printing system that imperiled the paper's efforts; the overheated newspaper scene in Bangkok had inflated itself beyond any probable capacity to sustain two such energetic English language newspapers. Revenues held steady, but costs did not. What had been sustainable before became burdensome and debilitating. The pressures were never ending – more than any from Thanat Khoman or even the drunken delivery team. We barely made payroll many months. We trimmed expenses here and there and always there more ominous noises about major new reductions. Again and again. It was with only this in fearful mind that I reported one day to my own boss' office, standing exactly on the carpet upon which we had so recently slept, expecting to hear about new cutbacks, more attrition – and preparing my reflexive arguments against it. I carried proposals charting the small amounts that could be saved by slicing away pages here, nibbling at hiring there, postponing expenses and re-pacing payment schedules ...

Instead, I was told that the ownerships of the two English-language papers had gotten together and worked out a grand merger, sort of the way Germany used to merge with its neighbors, an unequal amalgam with the Bangkok Post very much on top. The Bangkok World would be reduced to an afternoon edition only, Monday through Saturday. The magazine, the daily specials were finished. In fact, as I would be advised, the Bangkok World's news emphasis was to be changed entirely, diminished, downgraded, dismantled, in favor of light features, entertainment news, household advice and other such fluff as could be wrung from the wire services.

Uh, oh.

Where's Daw?

THERE WAS THIS CUTE LITTLE KID who sold sodas in the office. His name was Daw. He was always underfoot with his little wire tray of a dozen bottles of Coke or orange drink or Fanta or suspicious water and packets of dried fruit and cookies. He walked around like he owned the place, sliding into news sessions and business meetings or turning on his million-watt smile while you were on the phone, quite upending whatever you might have been talking about so seriously otherwise. Maybe he was eight years old; beyond any "maybe," he was as cute as a puppy. Every day I would buy a Coke from him – me twirling a baht coin high up into the air and, in our little ritual, him placing the bottle quickly before me and trying to catch the coin before it clattered to the floor. His eyes would flash brown joy as we watched the coin spin up and up and up. One time in ten he caught it and he would smile a smile that sang of the land's beauty, its essence, its bright spirit and happy pride. A sweet kid, Daw.

When the Bangkok Post guys took over, it became crystal clear that this was to be no amicable arrangement at all, and I guess it made sense that it wouldn't be. Although I had the strong, sad appreciation that we had lost, I didn't quite get it that they had won. But they were in charge and we were not. The paper was to be imploded, sections ended, staffers let go. We were to be told by the Post leaders who would be cut and how the new arrangement would play out. I knew it could never do for me; I had spent too much time competing with these mugs to be now working with them, working for them. They were businesslike enough and professional, yet it was so clear from my end that the Bangkok World was to be driven down, beaten down and that little good could come from that.

I had agreed to hang on, to help with the transition as the Post people moved in. That seemed the grown-up thing to do. Practically, I had another slight motive, too, less noble but vital to me nonetheless: I needed to get my money back. Most months of late, we had always seemed to come up short on the daily cash flow needed to make the payroll. The general manager, the easily offended Archarn Phayung, would wring his hands trying to come up with enough money to pay people. If he couldn't pull it off, I would give him cash from our small personal savings to tide us over until the end-of-the-month payments came in. He would then pay me back. Surely it offended all proper business practices to do things like that and maybe our casual approach to effective business practices is what landed us in such a pickle at the outset. What else could we do, though? People needed to be paid. They'd earned it, and it wasn't their fault that the paper was in such a state that the cash just wasn't there yet. That's all. It wasn't a tremendous amount – a thousand, fifteen-hundred dollars at a time, but it was pretty much all Pat and little Denis and I had. But even more than the money alone, I did want to help, to ease the new arrangement forward, to soften the blows if I could. In those early hours, I had the hope that maybe I could hold things together for a while, until the dust settled. Maybe vaingloriously, I thought that I had battled better than these guys and held the paper's own interests above water.

I could do that again, couldn't I? I could try. Didn't I owe the newspaper, owe my friends there, that? Who else would do it?

Emotions ran high but I tried to keep up the grim dance. Wasn't that what I had been doing for so long? Hadn't I glided away from angry authorities, juggled the scalding realities of the paper's finances for all this time? I could do this a bit longer. I just needed to keep my head, deflect some of the worst ideas, protect those who needed it, give up a little bit more here, work just a little harder there. I could do that.

AT ONE MORE MEETING, though, in the newspaper's small conference room, the Bangkok Post people were briskly outlining again and again for me, in tones such as you would use for daffy Uncle Charlie or a particularly dim child, some of the reductions and consolidations they were establishing, how they were recasting the editorial presence of the Bangkok World to a sliver of itself, designating what members of their staff would be on board and in charge to guide us simpletons on how to get out the paper. Even as I reeled under the force of the assault, I tried to hold on to the thought to keep quiet, trying to stop the nervous drumming drumming drumming of my fingers on the tabletop, that, yes, this is what happens and, yes, that I needed to keep as cool as I could to be able to help and ...

... and into the conference room sauntered a little kid, maybe eight years old, selling Cokes and sodas from his little wire basket. A cute little boy. But it wasn't Daw. I said, "Who is this? What happened to our kid?" Someone said, sort of absently, that he was the soda boy from the Post shop. They had brought him along. He'd be the one selling drinks here now.

Suddenly I went dizzy. I felt as if someone had hit me on the heart with a hammer. I couldn't get a word out. I couldn't think of anything to say, and it was all I could do to hold back tears. A grown man all misty-eyed. Imagine that. For all the huge losses in pride and dignity, the ghastly setbacks affecting so many noble efforts, so many wonderful people, so many dreams, it came down to the dumping of a little kid selling sodas to bring me so low. Clearly it showed. There was a huge deep silence to the room. Politely and in a gesture that I appreciate to this moment, Michael Gorman, the publisher of the Bangkok Post and a man who had always been friendly and open with me, stood up and said that maybe we needed to take a break, needed to digest what was to be done, needed to meet again tomorrow. They rose and, shooing the little boy ahead of them, quietly and, I think, kindly, left me entirely alone in the room, turning a baht coin over and over and over in my hand.

So very weary of the fight in that late summer of 1971, ground down by the unending pressures, the potshots from the government, saddened by the prospect of an unraveling of so much of what we had done, being baffled by all the changes in my own country that were turning all we knew upside down and, now, bested not by angry, coal-eyed police generals but by a new little kid selling the Cokes and cookies, the truth was dawn-clear to me.

It was time to go home.

Thereafter

IT TOOK MANY, MANY YEARS for us to return to Southeast Asia, half a generation before visiting once more the beauties of our earlier days. But back we came. Over several trips we came back to Bangkok, travelled through the north of Thailand once again. We went to Laos. To Burma. To Cambodia.

But not to Vietnam.

I could not bring myself to go to Vietnam. I twisted itineraries crazily to pass from one place to another without going to Vietnam, contorting air routes and the bankbook to fly, for example, from exquisite Luang Prabang to bruised-up Phnom Penh while avoiding, as if with my hands over my eyes, the Vietnam passing down beneath, when the plane actually stopped briefly on the way at Tan Son Nhat airport with Saigon in the near distance. It was no thing of fear or anxiety. There were no hauntings at all that I dreaded to face. It wasn't like that: it simply seemed wrong. Wrong to call in as a tourist where we had so purposefully killed and been killed, wrong to vacation in the echoes of even those distant, distant aches, wrong ambling about as if all that were somehow nothing now. I couldn't do it.

Of course I understood that it was a bit foolish of me. It was a far different time; we were far different people. The world had moved well on. After a time, as the nation has done with everyone except the

withered Cubans, Americans have turned away from our old harsh-
nesses and bloodshed and engaged yet again with our once-enemies.
Our companies do business where our soldiers fought. Poppies grow
in flanders' fields. People visit Gettysburg and Normandy, Japan and
Sicily and, yes, Vietnam, sometimes just for the fun of it. Not me for
Vietnam, although it made no great sense. So often I go to other places
of America's military pain and that of others: Germany. France. The
American South. Russia. China. Indian reservations. The Middle
East. Panama. Belgium. Cuba. Places where battles had been fought
as furiously as some around the South China Sea. Yet I didn't want to
return to Vietnam.

But then later – so much later; four full decades since we'd first
set foot in Southeast Asia –we pulled together yet another trip to the
region, bringing along two of our sons, Timothy and Daniel. I wanted
them to sense more of Thailand, to see more of a land that was so vital
to us, more of a culture that won our hearts before they were even
born. I booked us in for Cambodia, too, so that they could learn of
astonishing Angkor – and of the killing world of Pol Pot. Trying to
look at it as how they might be better served rather than just how I
might be most comfortable, I stared at the map for long hours. Thinking. Working once again the airlines, the travel guides, the hotels, I
could sense the melting away, the relenting. We went to Thailand. We
went to Cambodia. We went to the Socialist Republic of Vietnam, top
to bottom.

As easily as if we were dropping in on Des Moines, we flew from
Bangkok to Hanoi. Hanoi! I couldn't believe it. I was simply amazed
that I was there, walking those bustling streets. We wandered around
the austere, Spartan capital, saw the modest Ho Chi Minh's Tomb,
in which he likely spins at the very idea that there is a Ho Chi Minh's
Tomb at all so against his wishes, dodged the millions of motorbikes,

went to temples and markets exactly as if it were just any other fasci-natingly amazing place on the planet – rather than, as it was, Hanoi in the north of Vietnam. We rode in a little boat through the odd, other-worldly rocks of Halong Bay, admired the artists' work everywhere in little shops along quiet streets in wilting Hoi An. We worked our way down the cobra shaped country through places whose names existed to me from distantly long ago only as targets on some bomber's map, through landscapes where huge and small battles had been fought over and over. We stayed in the soothing, inviting, caressing ancient capital of Hue, where it risked having the stern authorities called to get me to move on to the next place, to leave that shaded, welcom-ing town where the women so memorably ride on bicycles in lovely ao dais, simple and simply beautiful silk tunics and trousers which the Communists on their victory sought to ban, almost mad cause enough to reopen the fighting. They relented, wisely. They might as well have commanded that the flowers have no petals. And in Vietnam I saw that the country is so very beautiful, something I barely knew from when it was bases and airfields and treetops that I saw. People were so nice, friendly, welcoming, something I had hardly appreciated back when gauging people took into account risks and perils more than any charms and personalities, intelligences and cultures.

I had done it all wrong, of course. We should have returned to know and learn far earlier. It's not like I didn't have some money in the game. Sometimes I'm just pretty slow to get it right.

It was only in Saigon – or, formally, Ho Chi Minh City as about 12 people in the world actually say – that the wooziness came upon me, a dizzying aura that this was an electric place that I seemed to know; so much that was knowable jellyfish-floated just below the surface, not in hovering, gnatty detail, an unformed sensation so familiar even if call-ing up auras from a quick and shallow but vital experience so very long before. This was the city of then, no matter how new now. Rushing, pushy, extravagant, edgy, audacious Saigon. It could make you laugh in its brashness. Feeling that we must stand out like ostriches, in fact hardly anyone paid much attention to us at all; I surely only imagined that it might seem, now and again, that older men, men of my own age, held a passing eye-lock an instant longer than did the hurryhur-ryhurry younger ones of today's world. Woozy, I had to leave the War Remnants Museum – opened long earlier as the "Exhibition House for US and Puppet Crimes" – because the effect and the emotions, the memories, were simply too powerful. I became purely shaken, short-breathed at the many photographs and exhibits – not just from those of "US and Puppet Crimes," although there were some of such, but especially at the youth and danger and ultimate pain captured in those fresh young American faces in those huge pictures, seeming so much younger than I was ever allowed to be.

But that was mostly me, once again. The Vietnamese weren't anywhere so interested in my baggage as I was. Fair enough, too. In all things we found the Vietnamese to be quite unobsessed with the American War, as they think of it, in its place with so many of their other wars. Of course they are very deeply and personally engaged with its reality, but they have other things to do now, different worries to master. Today is today.

We had a young guide in Saigon who, like two-thirds of the coun-try, like Tim and Dan traveling with us, was not born until the war was pretty much done or gone entirely. We seldom talked about those times except as he would tell us of so many, many wars the Vietnamese had fought to wrest their independence back from others. Wars with France, with China, with the Khmers, with the Americans. Like us, they fought so many wars – but they didn't have to travel to distant places to find one. He understood that I had been to Vietnam before but never much mentioned it directly. No one did. They were too polite for that. But one evening we were having dinner and we talked, cautiously, generally, about the war times. After a pause, he asked us if it were possible for us to send him books from America.

Books?

"Yes, history books, if you could. Not difficult books such as they have in universities; my English is not good enough for that," he said in his quite excellent English. "Maybe something that you use to teach the small children about those days. I would like to read that. You see," he said to me, to Denis Edward Horgan, "for the war, I know why we were here. I do not know why *you* were here."

Good question. Such a good question.

I DIDN'T TELL THAT YOUNG MAN that there were no lessons at all taught to our young children in their history books about the mighty American war in Vietnam. None. How could I explain to him that that terrible time has been folded into history's laundry and has been so largely ignored? There is no Vietnam, except where it exists as a metaphor for use by those usually making points quite disconnected to the realities of the war, or as a label, as a curse, as a badge. It is a coded event we were supposed to have learned from, at best. It is a scalding definition to apply to some poor soul who commits a crime or is found drunk and homeless – 40 years after. Lacking triumph, it is diminished as an important endeavor even as its consequences and casualties pain to this very instant in so many thousands of still-mourning hearts. Just another war – one followed soon enough by our bloody troubles in the Middle East, Grenada, Panama, the Balkans, Iraq, Afghanistan, Iraq again, Libya and more.

Pat and beautiful little Denis and I left Southeast Asia late in the summer of 1971 and it would be long decades, a quarter-century, before we would come back again. The love of the place hardly faded, though, but, rather, steadily grew more golden in the way that memories do, when uncluttered by wake-up realities and the sight of time's wrinkles and the truth's footprints overtreading the images that had been so burnished within recollection's and fantasy's mist. We had no money for such vast travel for a long, long time. We had these two more sons born at their own auspicious moments in the United States, and a brood so lively wasn't moved around the planet casually. There was so much else to discover as interests, jobs and fate moved us here and there. But we eventually did get to go back, cheerily feeling as awkwardly out of place in the new Asia as I did in the new America to which I had returned long before without a job, without much money but enriched beyond measure in memories and experience.

Not that many cared.

BECAUSE I DIDN'T REALLY KNOW what to expect I probably wasn't overly surprised that so few seemed to credit at all that I had dedicated so much time to working in such an exotic assignment as life handed us in Southeast Asia. I sensed, even, that it was held against me in some quarters, that I had somehow been frivolous or self-indulgent in dabbling in such distant waters when, it was thought, all that truly counted at all was to be found unfolding in the home of the brave and the land of the free.

That I had served the country as a soldier was not at all rare; millions of others had done so also. That simply was the way it was then. The war in Vietnam, fully exposed as a monstrous thing hatched in lies and blood-drenched misjudgment, had become something of an embarrassment and those who were ordered to carry it out often were confused with the policy itself, sharply less respected than even the most minimal standards of national honor would seem to insist upon. But the gang from Korea had gone through that, too. There aren't streets enough for the necessary parading that should conclude such service, particularly because the service might have been dedicated to so flawed a cause; so there was so little parading instead. You could hear that returning soldiers and Vietnam veterans were forced to endure scorn and derision but I never saw any of that nor ever met anyone who has, and consider it to be very much akin to the alligators in the sewers of urban myth. The idea, promulgated by the draft-evading Right, that the draft-evading Left would get confrontational with tough soldiers they believed to be homicidal lunatics, seems a bit daft as it probably wouldn't make a lot of sense for anyone to get particularly confrontational with tough, competently homicidal lunatics. Of course there was a great deal of flag-waving in those days, too, waving the flag being a neat dodge to mask the truth that the waving was most often done from where it was the safest and soundest. Soldiers, of course, were no more uniformly monsters or fools in those days than they are uniformly heroes and demigods today, all lead by modern Pattons and Alexanders the Great, so dubbed by reporters and barstool Rambos who wouldn't know a good officer from all the others. As in Thailand, the tin medals and badges still dazzle critical judgment everywhere.

Soldiering was something of a wash, then, coming home. The newspaper work in distant Bangkok, the business experience, the travel, the culture sampling, was all colorful, to be sure, to a few easily distracted spirits but few at all credited it as worthy enough an element on the curriculum vitae to welcome it in an employee. I couldn't find work. The money was running thin. Had the Thai time been a huge mistake?

In fact, cheerily against all the odds and cross-currents, it was a Bangkok echo that rescued me, providing an opportunity to move forward so wondrously over the next three and half decades of newspapering – and life.

Out of a job, out of the journalism mainstream for an upending half-decade, rich with skills and knowledge that no one much wanted, I sifted and sorted among what contacts I had remaining, wondering if anyone had any ideas. None did. The Linen Group declined even to return my calls; apparently I must have failed them mightily while working like a donkey, like a kwai chom poo, for them so far away. Maybe I had. (Their nails must have especially needed buffing, leaving them too busy to raise even an eyebrow when I sought help to shake the tree for the small amount of money I needed returned to me; but Giorgio Berlingieri paid me from his own pocket when he heard of it. He just opened his wallet and counted out the cash from what he was carrying around, making me wonder whether I wasn't entirely in the wrong end of the business with my own mothy billfold.) The Boston Globe had no place for me. The U.S. economy was in a mess and papers weren't much hiring. My old pal President Nixon had imposed wage and price controls and companies were cautious, hunkered down in a harsh recession enough to be not much impressed by anything I might have to offer. Things were not looking so good at all.

But then a dime well-dedicated connected me up with an old pal from the Globe days, my reporting mentor when I was first an intern there. Jim Doyle had moved on from the Irish Gang on Morrissey Boulevard to be a political writer for The Evening Star in Washington. He had passed through Bangkok covering a presidential tour of Vietnam and beyond and we had shared gossip and war stories of the zaninesses at either ends of our work lives. I called Jim and wondered if he knew of anything that might shoo the wolf away from the door. He got back to me and said that the Star wasn't hiring but there might be some day-work available on the copy desk. What I should do, he said, was to check in with a Burt Hoffman, the assistant managing editor.

Jim would grease the ways as best he could.

So, it was off to that most beautiful place, Washington, the District of Columbia, where I arrived at The Evening Star for an interview with this Burt Hoffman fellow. Waiting uncomfortably, having not had much luck of late with interviews, I rehearsed my various approaches, hoping to catch the busy man's attention with some small emphasis on the little copy editing that I had committed over recent time, much of it under circumstances quite unlike anything to be found or needed at 225 Virginia Avenue, southeast. Even as I nervously started to introduce myself, stumbling around with my prepared remarks, Burt popped up from his desk and was on me like I owed him money. "Denis. How good to see you. How's Pat doing? And how's the baby? Look, we're not hiring but can you come in for a week's try-out on the copy desk? There's no job to try out for but it'll give you some money and maybe something'll open up. Great. Tell me about Bangkok. I can't thank you enough for all you did for me."

I am mortified to say that I had no idea who this guy was and why he was so friendly to me. Of course, I gingerly acted as if he, too, had been on my mind every second of the day and that he was my best pal in the whole Milky Way and how awful it is that we haven't seen each other for so long, etc., etc., etc. Turns out he, too, had passed through Thailand on a war trip and had some relatives out there we knew; we met, had dinner; I'd set him up with some hard-to-get briefings and interviews, filling him in on things he needed to know that kept him from going too far wrong with the baloney being sliced and served up as truth thereabouts. Newspapering is a small town, and I did that for lots of people. It was all a blur, but that was part of the secret handshake club courtesy that news guys have for one another. Seldom, though, was it so importantly returned.

Burt got me the try-out, which soon opened up to a job on the

Star's overnight national desk. Over the next decade, the paper moved from being the Evening Star to the Washington Star-News to the Washington Star to the Out-of-Business Washington Star. Its ownership went from that of a collection of families that had intermarried with the consequences of such, as in British nobility, then passing briefly to a Texas banker who soon sold us, lock, stock and ink barrel, to Time, Inc., heaven help us all. The company's texture changed so often that it was as if I had worked at many different newspapers without ever changing the ZIP code. At the Star of blessed memory, I variously became foreign editor, ran presidential campaign coverage, managed special editorial projects, was lifestyle editor and wrote a human interest column. As is my destiny, I fought with and/or revered the various bosses, battling notably with those sent down to run the newspaper when Time Inc. decided that the Washington bumpkins could hardly be trusted with such responsibility without guidance from the Big City Slickers. Burt Hoffman, who quit the Star after some battle or another with one his own bosses, eventually fell into the uplifting company of a Thai woman and helped with her restaurant businesses in northern Thailand, the world being such a small place.

The Washington Star went out of business in 1981 jettisoning some of the industry's very best journalists, quite cluttering up the prospects of such as me who likely was never exactly so regarded. In the way of these heavenly things, when The Star ceased to twinkle it was aptly described a very good newspaper; five years later it was A Great Newspaper; and in five years more it was hailed in memory as The Greatest Newspaper in the History of the Creation. I'm not quite sure it was all that but it was very wonderful indeed, and holds a very special place in so many hearts decades on.

There was no Washington job this time, no Jim Doyles or Burt Hoffmans to slip me the skeleton key to the Washington back door.

Better, I found myself working for the next quarter-century at the Hartford Courant, as an editor first but most of the grand time as a columnist, with all the ups and downs that the business insists upon inflicting as a prerequisite and qualification to play in its goofy schoolyard. There was no Thai connection to the Connecticut work, and what few people even knew of my life abroad, shrugged away my tales as if I were talking on and on, a daft Ancient Mariner, about some mad moments of fevery imagination. No one had ever heard of Jim Thompson. No one cared that I might have something special in mind, say, if I found a place in my reflections for images of small noodle shops rivaling the many-stared restaurants of a community or when I saw darks things as being as black as Asian hair or heard temple chants in the wind still. So be it and so it was. Over a long and vital time, itself rich with sparky characters, personal heights and professional careen, the Courant allowed us the steadiness of life and prospects to eventually return to Southeast Asia to visit later, when the kids, so well-nurtured in New England, were largely grown.

We've kept in touch with so many from that amazing Bangkok world, while, sadly, so many others have been harvested by history. General Black passed away in time as did Giorgio Berlingieri and most of the field marshals and the ambassadors we knew there. Far too many of the Thai and international staff of the Bangkok World are gone now. Jim Thompson is missing still. Sacha Casella went on to do important work with the United Nations High Commission for Refugees, helping to organize efforts on behalf of postwar Vietnamese exiles among other valuable services, and he has written brilliantly of it. Bill Harting returned to the Boston Globe where he became a visionary in the new age's razzle-dazzle alchemy bringing new editing, technologies and production processes to the newspaper roulette wheel. Surely, Bill is the only man on the planet Earth who has done so well to apply his bright uplifting ideas to the ancient craft in hand-set type and the most modern in electronic printing circles, too. And all in between. He continues to take the finest photographs in the world.

Narong Ketudat fought the great fight against Thai corruption long after his time at the Bangkok World, notably being hunted by the Thai police and Army for months for his sparky anti-junta ideas when the government oppression mounted madly after student uprisings in the 1970s, skipping from small hotel to small hotel to avoid arrest. He later founded magazines, high-end travel agencies, a top recording studio and runs an entire, gigantic university in Bangkok. (Knowing so much of Thai life, he tells the illustrative tale: "Our students wear uniforms, as is the custom. One day a delegation of young women came to me and nervously pleaded that they be allowed to update the skirts of the uniform which were in the letter A, in the fashion such as elementary schoolgirls wore. 'We are women, not children,' they said to me. I agreed. They could change the skirts. That was on a Friday. The very next Monday, every woman in the school – more than 7,000 – had modern, tighter skirts on. In one day!" In a Thai university, he says, maybe like any university, "you cannot get ten people to agree to do anything in a year. If the building is on fire, three will insist to leave by the window; two others will have a meeting to vote on going out the door and will debate leaving in three days. Two others will stay there and decline to leave at all ... Yet thousands of these skirts changed in *one school day*. Fashion is more powerful than the Army!") John Millington went forward to do a wide variety of significant work with the Council on Foreign Relations in New York and environmental causes before retiring to Connecticut, of all places.

Mechai Viravaidya continued his own gadflying, taking up the cause of population control – controversial only because Thai authorities wanted no part of it; they preferred instead a huge population to buttress against the Vietnamese. They got that all right, whether it can be afforded or not. Today the population is at 70 million, double what it was in our day. Mechai went into the bemused countryside to widely promote and demonstrate the art of using condoms. To this day, a condom there is familiarly called a "Mechai." He has opened a restaurant in Bangkok, called Cabbages and Condoms. Apasra Hongsakula, as beautiful as ever, more so even, continues on in Bangkok running, appropriately, a beauty empire, uncluttered from ever having laid eyes on me, who is so grateful to her for her inspiration.

So many others are still in Bangkok, writing or working in what careers amuse them. There are distinguished journalists and authors all over the globe now who have the Bangkok World on their resumes. There are also diplomats and officials who might have absorbed more about the values of patience and understanding from work in our newsroom than even from the grand universities and foreign service training corps. People flowed on with their lives, some back to their homelands or sought out new ones, enriched by time on Phrasumaine Road. Others saw it, maybe, as just another pretty stamp in their life's passport. What can never happen again for any of us or all of us, though, is for what we had in those incredible times to be ever repeated as it was then.

The Bangkok World itself, soldiered along for some more years, doing its best, and then was closed down entirely in 1987. I only happened to read about the end of the World, without either a bang or a whimper, on the Internet. We had been there in the last of its independent days, and are so saddened that it has gone.

WE HAD RETURNED TO AN AMERICA that had changed so extraordinarily in the few years that we were away that we practically needed a tutor to understand its new attitudes, its exuberant freedoms, its complex tones, its rubbery new rules. I guess by some tick-tocking standards, I am measured up as a child of the Sixties, but not at all in the sense that the term has come to signify. My Sixties were the early Sixties, the flop-over years from Ike's fifties, more than the later psychedelic Sixties of drugs, Russian sex and rock & roll, of protest, confrontation, of new passions unbridling and expectations replacing what were before, at best, crewcut daydreams. While most of all that was exploding into the commonplace, I was out of town. Considering my bad experiences with the narcotics of alcohol and nicotine, missing the hard drug explosion was probably a very good thing for me. I would have killed myself for sure. It was an amazing time, and I only Rip van Winkled back into it as best I could, often feeling a step behind – but wiser in different ways, maybe, however oddly I may have fitted in.

Older than the younger guys in ascension and younger than the older folks still leading the march, I was so often part of neither. I would hear people I loved and respected so much talk about Asia as if they were talking about life on the planets Pluto or Saturn, and there'd be a crackling in my spirit listening to soldiers mischaracterized, the Orient and its culture minimized, its aspirations and venerated lifestyles cartoonized.

It was an electric time, this new America we returned to, of so many social elements grinding up against one another: the established orders crumbling in the face of the blasting energies of relentless newness; it was a season of long-accepted rules and regimens being batted out of hand as simply unworthy, often for no other reason than that rules existed at all, this by the untested but fascinatingly light-footed hopeful sorts. It was an era of offending government administrations' getting thrown out the window, one after another, altered entirely by the balloting people and the rule of the law. Bold new sounds and expectation opened up irreparable cracks in the old ways to the point where it may well be that music and the demanding entitlements of youth did more to topple oppressive, starchy regimes elsewhere than did the old-fashioned bombs and rockets and musty policies of our own starchy leaderships.

It all is so heady to recall, that leaping back into the social and political rapids of what America was becoming then, so vibrantly a new place entirely – even decades before the Internet arrived to explode to smithereens any fantasies the fussy and reluctant oligarchs had of somehow going back to the old, patriarchal ways. So much was turned on its head and so quickly in those days; just riding that avalanche down the mountainside was its own brisk adventure.

I'm never quite sure whether the Asian time better prepared me to imagine the routes of the incredible change or, just as possibly, left me slightly less ready for its possibilities than were others. There was much to learn within a swirl where the small, sturdy steps of before weren't at all good enough anymore. No more incremental advances on civil rights, women's equality, acceptance of those who are different; tearing down the entire worm-ridden structure of intolerance was called for. No more satisfactions from important but ridiculously tiny developments, say, negotiating with the Soviets over some obscure number of counterclockwise engine gears in the nuclear arms race – when it was the collapse of the entire Soviet system itself that was taking place largely unseen and unanticipated, just around the corner.

What a time.

INTERESTINGLY, MY ODD ROLES in the Bangkok world, and the Bangkok World, were part of a pattern that would continue for me almost forever after in newsrooms, of me ending up in assignments I hadn't at all set out at all to achieve, of rising and falling on my capacity to meet challenges I had seldom signed up for in the first place. I felt like the baseball shortstop being judged for his skills manning someone else's hockey goal. I never planned in any meaningful way for being an Army officer, with any true understanding of what that actually meant. I certainly never tipped my cap towards being part of such a war as dominated my early years. I never set out to be a newspaper boss. Surely, I never had any desire to be engaged in a newspaper's business end. I never much even wanted to be an editor – writing and storytelling being my drug of choice instead. But those were the avenues that opened up when I most needed them, or was least able to resist. In Korat. In Bangkok. In Washington and Hartford. An editor? I could do that. If no one was wanting me to write, I slid into work by the editing door. A bit of professional pleasantry landed me an editing job in Washington, exactly when work was so very much needed, and, because it seems maybe I could do it well, editing is what I had to do for so long after.

They weren't looking for me to write in Hartford but left open the rear window to that with the chance to help edit the newspaper's Sunday magazine – and then barely noticed my crab-steps along the editing dance floor to where I was writing more and more, until there was little left to do with me, short of firing me, but to allow me to write what I so wanted: a column. I rose and slid, climbed and clung, through editing and managing responsibilities in the capitals of Thailand, the United States and the state of Connecticut, because the need for editors and managers was there and someone always seemed to imagine that I was the peg for the hole, often without looking too carefully at the shapes involved. But, truly, it wasn't what I had in mind, all this bossing about; it was writing that I had in mind. But I did what the paycheck commanded, always on the lookout for chances of change. Why, after Bangkok, would I ever think that that change wouldn't appear? And it always most wondrously and almost magically did.

As things took their phantasmagorical route, the certainty that there was a chance of change, a certainty spawned even before my Asian years but heightened so there, became an almost instinctive force in my calculations. I came to feel even more strongly that there was a spark already burning within even the most unsuspecting things that could even unknowingly but well work for me, when logic and other grumpy resources might insist otherwise. Lucky beyond any imagining, things so often had gone well for me, but only after Asia did I bank on it. I only had to get out of the way of its happening, this magic.

Back even before I became a newspaper guy, I paid for college by working nights in an ice company, running big rusting cranes which moved about huge molds in which froze large bars of ice – each cold slab weighing twice what I did in those slim times. Skinny and clumsy, I was expected to wrest those bars from their shells and push them, one by one, into the main ice house, using a long pole with hooks on the end. Each bar weighted three-hundred-and-twenty pounds. Eighteen of them in a row, or grid. Thirty-six rows or grids over a shift.

Possibly it was because of the thick ammonia fumes from the freezing solution, or more likely from the Pickwick Ale I drank while working, I somehow came to appreciate that if I thumped each heavy ice block just so, kicking it amidships and getting it to wobble, I could move that bar easily on its own energy rather than hoping, all 150 pounds of me, to haul such a weight by myself. It worked. I could get them to dance like dominoes. I am sure there is some physics hidden in all that, but what I came to know was that I could do this impossible thing by moving the energy rather than moving the ice.

So much of what small successes I might have committed managing people over time as a newsroom boss, and which kept my own bosses from hurling me out the high corporate windows, came from that understanding that the energy was already there, often needing but the slightest assistance for it to succeed. Appreciating the rhythms of authority in newsrooms and in the Army, I understood that there was such a strong power of spirit and talent and knowledge and willingness already in those around me. The easy trick was to smooth the channel for it. The very worst bosses I saw were those who tried to force people, through brusqueness and blind command, to do things differently than they often could do quite well on their own. The very best bosses I saw were those who, like the little broom people in the silly sport of curling, almost invisibly made it possible for the great mass of talent, like the bars of ice, to move of its own force, assisted with just the right guidance, pressure, understanding, inspiration, a thump amidships.

At the Bangkok World, in particular, the energy came in so many international flavors, from such remarkably uneven traditional journalistic backgrounds, that no amount of strutting about could, by itself, be hoped to marshal that force forward against the grain. There – and exactly as it should be pretty much everywhere – what had succeeded over the centuries and over the years at 522 Phrasumaine Road was a culture so much better built for the long, gentle haul. Certainly it required a bit of diplomacy here, a touch of silver-tongued persuasion there; it demanded rules and process, authority and steadiness, but, more, a patience and a capacity to roll with the results which sometimes would go so very far astray. But, because there would be another paper tomorrow and the tomorrow to follow, the better hope would be to train, to improve, to explain, to appreciate. Appreciating that would guide me anywhere, everywhere.

Obvious? Maybe. But everything then was so new to me that I

seized on anything that would help others do their best to get the work done, and to learn from them in the doing of it. And the paper did come out every day, even as any whirling, chugging computer could analyze the prospects and predict that such was surely impossible.

BUT THIS IS ALL FAR DEEPER and way beyond where my tale of the Bangkok World needs to be. The archaic, exotic mechanics of Bangkok newspapering is gone forever. Never again will we see such as that. But the professional essence of those who worked the wooden floors there can be found at a thousand computer keyboards today. The energy and sense of the bizarre that defined so many in Bangkok enlivens so many now at a thousand other new and baffling endeavors.

Ah, but it was surely an amazing time, setting me on the path to welcoming each new day's new amazement since. The memories, the experiences, the stories that still come back over me like the surf, always prepare me for the fresh roads to follow – each, too, vibrant and earth-twirling, but, truth be told, maybe having to struggle to be quite so special as from those wondrous times long ago in Thailand.

We worked hard, but we had so much fun, too. Opportunity, as it will, blossomed where it seemed that nothing so rich could possibly grow. Adventure arose, as it always will, pointing to new adventures still yet to arrive. How could we ever capitulate to the bleak prospects, of an imagined boredom, when such excitement is always just at the horizon? Improbably, in Bangkok, the puzzle pieces came together to create a stupendous experience, a time so exactly right in satisfaction and accomplishment and joy. It was a moment both unique and universal, that special spot along the planet's long arc. But why would we ever think that such as that is exhausted?

Bangkok taught that when the heart has been so astonishingly opened, how can I fear that it will narrow down, fall small and tight?

Loving a people who believe things differently than I believe, how could I ever think, then, that what I believe is the only thing to believe? It cannot ever happen exactly that way again, nor should it; but that hardly means that no such adventure or mystery and joy can ever happen again, nor that we should give up looking for it, awaiting it, welcoming it. Those times are both done and unendable. There are, exactly, in so many fresh new hearts everywhere, every moment, similarly intense awakenings of the senses, absorbing the sparkle of their own new sounds, the flashes of fresh color and history and culture; for spirits eager to receive them, the same laughter waits with the wind, the same light and sparkle are in the breeze.

The river, all the rivers, of our lives may sometimes just seem dull, cluttered with the unscraped tankers and heavy-shouldered freighters of necessity; but to know that someday, any day soon, there will appear again true grandeur such as the king's great royal barge procession – the Narai Song Suban – in full pageant, gold and jasmine, serpent heads and lotus bells glittering in the sun, hundreds of white helmeted oarsmen in perfect flow, is to know that there is forever beauty to come. All else stops to see that. And, yes, the fields, all our fields, can seem flat and dusty, speaking only of hard work for small gain and only more difficult effort to forever follow; but we can know that the path can turn a corner and there is a village temple, white walls, green and red-orange in the roof tiles, bells a-tinkling up in the golden eaves somewhere and where the good monks glide along the walkways, accepting our gifts, giving the gift of giving. It has happened and it will happen again.

I know this is so because I have seen it. The door of the past always remains ajar to bow in the future – in Bangkok's world, or anywhere we open our hearts. We need only listen for the soft footfalls of the chingchok.

About the Authors

DENIS HORGAN is a veteran journalist and author who has worked for newspapers in Boston, Massachusetts, Dublin, Ireland, Washington, D.C., Hartford, Connecticut, and as editor of the Bangkok World in Thailand. He has been an Army officer, a reporter, an editor, a columnist, a publisher and a copy boy. Beyond his journalism, he has written books of essays, fiction, short stories and, now, memoir. He was born in a taxicab.

Also by Denis Horgan:
Sharks in the Bathtub
Flotsam: A Life in Debris
The Dawn of Days
Ninety-Eight Point Six ... and other stories

IF THERE WAS ONE THING William Harting learned at college, it was that he didn't want to end up working for a newspaper. But he did, as a reporter and editor at Northeastern University, later in Quincy, Massachusetts, in Boston and as managing editor of the Bangkok World. They're the same anywhere. As much as the significance of the printed page, he is fascinated by the mechanics of the process, and that the one can't exist without the other. He is equally fascinated with the ability of a photograph to tell a story, and continues to practice that art. He was not born in a taxicab.

Also by William Harting:
Floating in place
Assorted Colors and Sizes
Just a Moment

THIS BOOK was designed by Elias Roustom, the master printer at EM Letterpress in New Bedford, Massachusetts, in close consultation with the writer and the photographer. The inspiration for the layout and the typography of this edition was taken directly from studying archival issues of The Bangkok World which unlike modern newspapers was a wide broadsheet, roughly mimicked by the proportions of this book. As the text for The Bangkok World was hand-set in a variety of foundry types, most notably Gill Sans for the headlines and Times for the copy, this edition uses Adobe Gill Sans Bold for the chapter headings and Font Bureau Starling Book for the copy. The book cover design uses a colored screen of a William Harting photograph depicting workers in the composing room, as a background texture, and uses colors and imagery inspired by the full color Sunday magazine published along with The Bangkok World.

AT THE BEGINNING of this book is a Thai inscription from the ancient capitol at Sukhothai, evoking life in the benevolent reign of King Ramkhamhaeng, which translates to:

Whoever wishes to trade horses, so trades.
Whoever wishes to trade elephants, so trades.
In the water there is fish. In the field there is rice.

บัตรประจำตัว

ผู้สื่อข่าวต่างประเทศ

PRESS CARD

ลายเซ็นผู้ถือบัตร
(Signature)

THANK YOU to so many without whom this wonderful experience mightn't have made it to the page, and beyond. Of course, deep appreciation to Bill Harting who inspired the project and for his kindness, age-long friendship, unending example and gracious presence over such a wonderful lifetime. Thank you to Patricia Horgan for providing the sustaining spark to my life's very core – and for her keen-eyed editing, tough standards and warm understanding. Also, to Timothy Horgan for anticipating the opportunities in allowing a corner of his Bluefoot creative world to embrace literary efforts, to Denis Horgan Jr. for his encouragement and for building a webpage to carry this book to the distant reaches of the Internet, and to Bluefoot's Angie Pierandri for her caring professionalism and unflagging diligence in getting this work before its audience and arranging the complexities of its marketing. Without these and more, this Bangkok experience might very well have glimmered only quietly in memory.